KHANIQAHI-NIMATULLAHI

(NIMATULLAHI SUFI ORDER)

306 West 11th Street
New York, New York 10014
Tel: 212-924-7739

11019 Arleta Avenue
Mission Hills, Los Angeles,
California 91345
Tel: 818-365-2226

4021 19th Avenue
San Francisco,
California 94132
Tel: 415-586-1313

4642 North Hermitage
Chicago, Illinois 60640
Tel: 312-561-1616

4931 MacArthur Blvd. NW
Washington, D.C. 20007
Tel: 202-338-4757

405 Greg Avenue
Santa Fe, New Mexico 87501
Tel: 505-983-8500

84 Pembroke Street
Boston,
Massachusetts 02118
Tel: 617-536-0076

219 Chace Street
Santa Cruz, California 95060
Tel: 408-425-8454

310 NE 57th Street
Seattle, Washington 98105
Tel: 206-527-5018

95 Old Lansdown Road
West Didsbury, Manchester
M20 8N2, England
Tel: 061-434-8857

41 Chepstow Place
London W2 4TS,
England
Tel: 01-229-0769

SUFISM IV

Also available by Dr. Javad Nurbakhsh

SUFISM IV

Repentance
Abstinence
Renunciation
Wariness
Humility
Humbleness
Sincerity
Constancy
Courtesy

by

Dr. Javad Nurbakhsh

KHANIQAHI - NIMATULLAHI PUBLICATIONS
LONDON   NEW YORK

Translated by William Chittick.

British Library Cataloguing in Publication
Repentance, abstinence, renunciation,
  wariness, humility, humbleness, sincerity,
  constancy, courtesy. —— (Sufism;4).
  1. Sufism
  I. Nurbakhsh, Javad, 1927 - II. Series
  297' .4

ISBN 0-933546-33-5

Published by Khaniqahi-Nimatullahi Publications
41 Chepstow Place
London W2 4TS
England
Telephone: 01-229-0769

Distributed by:
Kegan Paul International Ltd.
11 New Fetter Lane
London EC4P 4EE

Printed by Morning Litho Printers Ltd. in Great Britain (TU)
Tel: 01-474-3801

TABLE OF CONTENTS

ABBREVIATIONS USED IN THE TEXT

(Full bibliographical information on these works may be found in the bibliography)

AA	Bākharzi. *Aurād al-ahbāb wa fosus al-ādāb*
AM	Foruzānfar. *Ahādith-e Mathnawi*
AT	Ebn ol-Monawwar. *Asrār at-tauhid*
B	Sa'di. *Bustān*
EM	Ebn Māja. *as-Sonan.*
EO	Ghazāli. *Ehya' 'olum ad-din*
FM	Ebn 'Arabi. *al-Fotuhāt al-makkiyya*
HAu	Jāmi. *Haft aurang*
JS	Soyuti. *al-Jāme 'as-saghir*
KF	Tahānawi. *Kashshāf Estelāhāt al-fonun*
KM	Hojwiri. *Kashf al-mahjub*
KST	*Kholāsa-ye Sharh-e Ta'arrof*
KW	Kāshāni. *Kashf al-wojuh*
LT	Sarrāj. *al-Loma' fe 't-tasawwof*
M	Rumi. *Mathnawi*
MA	Ruzbehān. *Mashrāb al-arwāh*
MH	Kāshāni. *Mesbāh al-hedāya*

ix

MO   Bertels. *Mer 'at al 'oshshāq*.

MS   Anṣāri. *Manāzel as-sa'erinin*

NO   Jāmi. *Nafahāt al-ons*

RA   Tabrizi. *Rashf al-alhāz*

RAS Anṣāri. *Majmu 'a-ye resā 'el*

RJ   Jonaid. *Fe 'l-farq*

RQ   Qoshairi. *ar-Resālatat al-Qoshairiya*

RSh Shāh Ne'mato'llāh. *Rasā 'el*

S   Ghazāli. *Sawāneh*

SB   Bokhāri. *us̱-Sahih*

SD   Dāremi. *as-Sonan*

SGR Lāhiji. *Sharh-e Golshan-e rāz*

SM   Anṣāri. *Sad maidān*

SMS Moslem. *as̱-Sahih*

ST   Termedhi. *as-Sonan*

T   Kalābādhi. *at-Ta 'arrof*

TA   'Aṭṭār. *Tadhkerat al-auliā'*

TFA Anṣāri. *Tafsir-e 'erfāni wa adabi*

TJ   Jorjani. *at-Ta 'rifāt*

TSA Anṣāri. *Tabaqāt aṣ-ṣufiya*

TSS Solami. *Tabaqāt aṣ-ṣufiya*

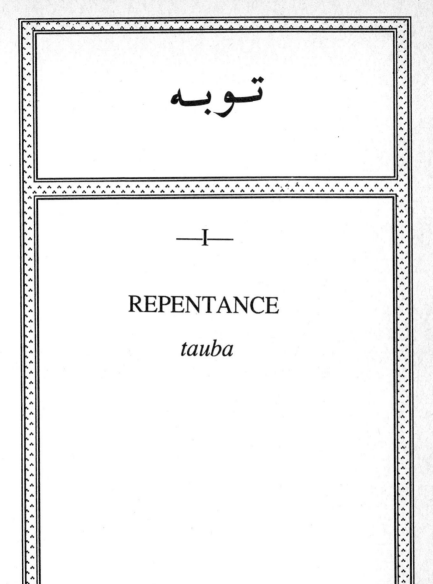

توبه

—I—

REPENTANCE

tauba

Our wine-drinking
gives life to the Tavern of Ruin,
our neck pays the blood price
of two thousand repentances.
I repent,
then break my repentance,
because Mercy gains splendor
from my sinning.

S 295

From the point of view of the Shari'at, "repentance"
(*tauba*)is to turn away from acts of disobedience (*ma.'ā-
si*) and sins (*dhonub*). In the technical vocabulary of
the sufis, it is to turn away from everything that
displeases God and toward everything that pleases Him.
The repentance of beginners is to turn away from
improper actions, that of intermediates to turn away from
inappropriate thoughts and intentions, and that of the
advanced to turn away from their own existence in the
face of Absolute Being.

1

DIVERGENCES AMONG THE MASTERS
IN DESCRIBING REPENTANCE

In describing and evaluating repentance, the sufi masters have provided a variety of definitions.

Hojwiri writes:

Sahl ebn 'Abdo'llāh and a group of others say, "Repentance is that you never forget your sin"; rather, you should be upset about it constantly, so that you do not become self-satisfied through your good works, even if they are many. Regret for bad actions takes precedence over good actions. Can a person who does not forget his sins ever be self-satisfied?

But Jonaid and another group say, "Repentance is that you forget your sin." He who repents is a lover, the lover is in witnessing (*moshāhadat*), and the remembrance of unfaithfulness (*jafā'*) in witnessing is unfaithfulness. For a time he will be with unfaithfulness, and then for a time with the remembrance of unfaithfulness; but the remembrance of unfaithfulness veils kindliness.

This difference of opinion goes back to a disagreement over spiritual struggle (*mojāhadat*) and witnessing, a disagreement which is mentioned in [the chapter of this book on] the position of Sahl and his followers.[1] Those who say that a person repents through his own self consider his forgetting of sin as heedlessness (*ghaflat*), but those who say that he repents through God maintain that his remembrance of sin is to associate others with God (*sherk*). In short, if the repenter's own attributes subsist, the knot of his

1. See R.A. Nicholson, *The Kashf al-Mahjūb: The Oldest Persian Treatise on Sufism*, London, 1970, pp. 200 ff.

inmost consciousness (*serr*) will not have been untied; but if his own attributes have been annihilated, he should not remember his attributes. Moses said, "I have repented toward Thee" (VII:143) in the state where his attributes subsisted; the Prophet said, "I cannot count Thy praises"[1] in the state where his attributes had been annihilated.

In short, remembrance of alienation in the place of nearness is alienation; the repenter must not remember his own selfhood — so how should he remember his sins? In fact, to remember sins is a sin, since it is an instance of turning away. Just as sin is an instance of turning away, so also remembering it is an instance of turning away, and remembering anything else is the same. Just as remembering a crime is a crime, so also forgetting it is a crime, since both remembering and forgetting are tied to you. Jonaid said, "I have read many books, but none gave me as much profit as this:

"When I said, 'I did not sin,'
    She said in reply,
'Your life is a sin
    to which no other sin can compare.'"

Since the existence of a lover in the presence of a lover is a pollutant, what value can describing him have?

KM 381-382

1. Allusion to a famous supplication of the Prophet: "I take refuge in Thy approval from Thy anger and in Thy pardon from Thy punishment. I take refuge in Thee from Thee. I cannot count Thy praises — Thou art as Thou hast praised Thyself" (SMS, Salat 222; SD, Salat 148; ST, Da'awat 75,112; ect.).

3

Jonayd was asked, "What is repentance?" He replied: "That you forgetyour sin." To forget the sin is for its sweetness to leave your heart, such that no trace of it remainsin your awareness. You become as if you had never committed it. In other words, God's great ness and awesomeness fall into your inmost consciousness because you were unfaithful, and you become so occupied with that greatness and awesomeness that you do not remember unfaithfulness; after that it never occurs to you that it would be fitting to act unfaithfully.

KST 275

THE ROOT OF REPENTANCE

The root of repentance lies in the restrictions laid down by God, the awakening of the heart from the sleep of heedlessness, and its vision of its present defects. When the servant of God meditates upon his own bad states and ugly actions and seeks to be rid of them, God makes it easy for him to repent, releases him from the misfortune of his disobedience, and takes him to the sweetness of obedience *(ṭā 'at)*.

KM 380

REPENTANCE COMES FROM GOD

How long must we burn like incense
    in the fire of repentance?
Pour out the wine,
    for a lifetime has passed in unripe madness.

Ḥāfeẓ

4

In short, repentance is divine confirmation, while acts of disobedience are corporeal activities. When remorse enters the heart, the body has no organ with which to repel it. Since the body's acts cannot repel relentment at the beginning, so also they cannot preserve repentance in the end. The Koran says, "Then God relented toward Adam — verily He is Ever-Relenting, All-Compassionate" (II:37)."[1]

KM 382

It was said to our master [Abu Saʻid Aboʼl-Khair], "So-and-so repented and then broke his repentance." He replied, "If relentment had not broken with him, he would never have broken repentance."

AT 296

A man said to Rābeʻa, "I have sinned a great deal. If I repent, will God relent toward me?" She replied, "No, but if He should relent toward you, you will repent."

RQ I 324

CONFIRMING REPENTANCE IS UNNECESSARY

> Repentance in its firmness
>   seemed like a stone —
> Look how easily the wineglass
>   smashed it!

Ḥāfeẓ

You should know that repentance does not necessarily have to be confirmed. If a repenter,

1. The word *tauba* or "to repent" is applied in Arabic and Persian to both God and man; when it refers to God we translate it as "to relent".

5

deciding not to return to disobedience, should lapse and return to disobedience, his repentance during those past days must be judged to have been correct and he will reap its reward. There have been beginners and repenters among the sufis who have repented and then lapsed, returning to ruin; but then they have come again to the Threshold because of being admonished.

One of the masters — God have mercy on them — has said, "I repented seventy times and then returned to disobedience; the seventy-first time I found constancy."

Abu 'Amr Nojaid said, "In the beginning I repented at the session of Abu 'Othmān Ḥiri and held fast to my repentance for a time. Then something in my heart called me to disobedience and I followed it, turning away from companionship with this master. Whenever I saw him from afar I would become upset and flee lest he catch sight of me. One day I met him suddenly. He said to me, 'My son, do not remain the companion of your enemies, unless you are impeccable. For an enemy will see your defects, and when you have faults, he will be happy. But if you should be impeccable, he will be sad. If you must commit acts of disobedience, come to us so that we may suffer your affliction and your enemy will not be made happy.' With this my heart became sick of sin and my repentance was put in order."

I have also heard that a person repented of acts of disobedience and afterwards returned to them. Then he became remorseful. One day he said to himself, "If I should return to the Threshold, what sort of state will I have?" A voice spoke from the Unseen World: "You obeyed Us, so We showed you gratitude; then you left Us, so We gave you respite. If you return to Us

6

We will accept you."

THE PRECONDITIONS FOR REPENTANCE

The Prophet said, "Remorse is repentance." In these words the preconditions for repentance are summed up: One precondition is regret for opposition [to God's commandments], a second is the immediate abandonment of lapses, and a third is firm determination not to return to disobedience. All three preconditions are tied to remorse and regret, since, when remorse is present in the heart, the other two preconditions follow upon it.

Remorse has three causes, just as repentance has three preconditions. First, when the fear of punishment comes to rule the heart and grief over bad actions takes shape within it, this results in remorse. Second, the desire for favors seizes the heart and it becomes obvious that they cannot be acquired through evil acts and disobedience, so the person has regrets, hoping that they will come. Third, he experiences shame before God and regrets his opposition. In the first case the person is 'repentant' (*tā'eb*) in the second 'penitent' (*monib*), and in the third 'continually repenting' (*awwāb*).[1]

THE FIRST STAGES OF REPENTANCE

Three states must be considered the first stages of repentance : Arousal (*tanbih*), disquiet (*zajr*), and

1. For an explanation of these three degrees of repentance, which are founded upon three different Koranic terms, see below, 'The Stations of Repentance', p. 14.

7

guidance *(hedāyat)*. Arousal is a state that settles into a person's heart at the beginning of repentance. It awakens him from the sleep of heedlessness and makes him see the error of his path and his own misguidance. Disquiet is a state which makes him uneasy about his staying and going forward in error and misguidance; it prods him to seek the Straight Path. Guidance is a state which shows that he has found the Straight Path. He is like a traveler who has lost the road and slept in the trackless wastes, when suddenly a guide arrives, awakening him and urging him to leave the wastes and head for the road, thereby bringing him to the path.

MH 366-67

THE ALLIES OF REPENTANCE

Repentance is allied with four things: Seeing the defects of acts, guarding *(re'āyat)*, self-examination *(mohāsabat)*, and meditation *(morāqabat)*.

'Seeing the defects of acts' is for the person never to look upon any of his own acts with admiration; rather, he must see them as defective and incomplete. And how should the acts of beginners be anything but defective? For their acts are never empty of the stains of [sensual] gratification *(hazz)*.

'Guarding' is constantly to protect and preserve one's outward and inward self from intending or inclining toward opposition [to God's commands], for just as disobedience is an outward sin, taking pleasure in remembering it after having refrained from it is an inward sin.

'Self-examination' is constantly to study and investigate the acts and states of one's own self. One

8

must enumerate and list the conformities and oppositions that arise from it day by day, or rather hour by hour. Through their increase and decrease one becomes aware of the nature of one's own state.

'Meditation' is for the person to see that God observes and examines him in all outward movements and stillnesses and in all inward thoughts and intentions. Just as he is cautious of acts of disobedience outwardly and is ashamed of them, so he guards against blameworthy thoughts inwardly and is ashamed of them. Thus his outward and inward become constant in repentance.

MH 367-68

THE PILLARS OF REPENTANCE

Repentance has five pillars: Performing obligatory acts *(adā-ye farā edh,* making up for what has slipped by *(qadhā-ye mā fāt),* seeking the lawful *(talab-e halāl),* making restitution for misdeeds *(radd-e mazālem),* and struggling with and opposing the *nafs*[1]*(mojāhadat wa mokhālafat bā nafs).*

'Performing obligatory acts' is to observe all commands and prohibitions made obligatory by the Shari'at in their appointed times.

'Making up for what has slipped by' is to make up for every [obligatory] act that was missed in past time.

'Seeking the lawful' is to purify one's food, drink and clothing from the stains of being unlawful or doubtful, since purifying them has a tremendous effect

---

1. *Nafs* signifies literally 'soul' or 'self', but in sufi terminology it refers to the tendency within man that turns him away from God, the sum total of his egocentrism, ignorance, blind passion, and every other negative attribute.

9

upon purifying the inward self.

'Making restitution for misdeeds' is to clear oneself of obligation for others' rights and to mend the fractures of injustice and transgression by compensation and reparation. If the misdeed should be in respect of property, the person should restore it; if it should be a crime such as killing, wounding, striking, vilifying, backbiting, or defaming, he should clear his obligation through submitting to retaliation, indemnity, or payment.

'Struggling with and opposing the *nafs*' is to discipline it by weaning it from familiar things and curbing it from passions; as a result the person becomes accustomed to refrain from physical pleasures and achieves detachment. He no longer enjoys recalling the familiar unlawful things which he has outwardly forgone and rejected and of which he has repented; his outward and inward self become constant in repentance and he becomes patient and satisfied in performing commanded acts and refraining from everything prohibited.

MH 368-369

THE RESULTS OF REPENTANCE

The results of repentance are four:

God's love: "Truly God loves those who repent" (II:222).

Being cleansed of sins: "He who repents of sins is like him who has no sins."[1]

The changing of evil deeds into good deeds:"[Save him who repents, has faith, and does righteous actions]

1. The saying is a *hadith* and is cited by Ghazāli, Soyuti and others (cf. AM 167).

10

those, God will change their evil deeds into good deeds"
(XXV:70).

Being singled out for the prayers of the angels who
carry God's Throne: "[Those who bear the Throne...
ask forgiveness for those who have faith: 'Our Lord...]
forgive those who have repented'" (XL:7).

MH 369

THE SIGNS OF REPENTANCE

Repentance has two signs:
Regret for what has slipped by and haste to
compensate for it.

According to a *hadith*, "Sins in God's eyes are to
make little of sins and to delay repentance." Shebli said,
"Delaying repentance is one of the greatest acts of
disobedience, for when the sinner says, 'I will repent in
a year,' the meaning is, 'I will disobey God for a year.'"

MH 369-70

THE LEVELS OF REPENTANCE

There are four levels of repentance:
Turning away from unbelief (*kofr*); this is the
repentance of the unbelievers

Turning away from prohibited activities, such as
ungodliness (*fesq*), lewdness (*fojur*), and acts of
opposition to the Shari'at; this is the repentance of the
ungodly.

Turning away from blameworthy moral traits
(*akhlā-e dhamima*) and ugly qualities (*ausāf-e qabiha*);
this is the repentance of the pious.

Turning away from everything other than God; this is

the repentance of the perfect among the prophets and the friends of God (*auliā'*)— upon them be peace!

SGR 258

At the beginning repentance is turning away from sins and evil deeds, then turning away from lapses and instances of forgetfulness, then turning away from seeing one's own good deeds and acts of obedience, then turning away from resting with any created thing; finally, it is to be at ease with the world of mystery and hidden things (*'ālam as-serr wa l-khafiyāt*). When one first arrives at a station (*maqām*), that is obedience, nearness (*qorb*), and witnessing; but when one passes beyond that station and moves forward, returning to it is a veil and disobedience.

KST 276

THE KINDS OF REPENTANCE

Repentance is of three kinds: From what is wrong (*khatā'*) to what is right (*sawāb*), from what is right to what is more right, and from what is right in one's own view to God.

'From what is wrong to what is right' follows from the Koran's words, "Those who, when they commit an indecency or wrong themselves, remember God and pray forgiveness for their sins ... and do not persevere in the things they did" (III:135).

'From what is right to what is more right' is found in Moses' words, "I repent to Thee" (VII:143).

'From self to God' is found in the Prophet's words, "My heart becomes clouded and I ask forgiveness from

12

God seventy times a day."[1]

To do something wrong is ugly and blameworthy, while to turn away from the wrong to the right is good and praiseworthy. This is the repentance of the common people, and its properties are obvious.

As long as the more right exists, remaining with the right is to come to a halt and be veiled. To turn away from the right to the more right is praiseworthy for those who have reached the degree of the people of aspiration (*ahl-e hemmat*). This is the repentance of the elect. After all, it is absurd for the elect to repent of disobedience. Do you not see that the whole world was burning with desire for the vision of God, yet Moses repented of that, since he asked for vision out of his own personal choice? But personal choice is a plague upon love. In order to refrain from that plague, he showed the creatures his refraining from vision.[1]

Turning away from self to God takes place in the degree of love. Just as one repents from halting at a high station because it is a plague upon a higher station, so one repents from seeing stations and states (*aḥwāl*). Thus the Prophet rose in station at every instant; when he reached a higher station, he asked forgiveness for the lower station and repented of looking upon it.

KM 383

1. The *ḥadith* is found in SMS (*Dhekr* 41) and other standard sources.
2. Reference to the Koranic account alluded to above: "Moses said [to God], 'Oh my Lord, show me, that I may behold Thee!' Said He, 'Thou shalt not see Me...', and Moses fell down swooning. So when he awoke, he said, 'Glory be to Thee! I repent to Thee' (VII: 143).

13

Repentance has three stations: Repentance, penitence, and continual repentance. The cause of repentance is the fear of punishment, of penitence the desire for reward, and of continual repentance the observation of God's command.

'Repentance' is the station of the common believers, who turn away from major sins, in accordance with the Koran's words, "O believers, repent to God with unswerving repentance" (LXVI:8).

'Penitence' is the station of God's friends and those brought near to Him (*moqarrabān*), in keeping with the Koranic passage, "Whosoever fears the All-Merciful in the Unseen and comes with a penitent heart" (L:33).

'Continual repentance' is the station of the prophets and emissaries, in keeping with the Koranic verse, "How excellent a servant! He was continually repenting" (XXXVIII: 30, 44).

So 'repentance' is to turn away from major sins through obedience, 'penitence' is to turn away from minor sins through love, and 'continual repentance' is to turn away from self to God. The difference between turning away from indecent acts to commands, from small sins and thoughts to love, and from selfhood to God is obvious.

KM 380

THE DEGREES OF REPENTANCE

The first degree is the repentance of those who perform actions; it is to turn from corrupt actions to good actions.

The second degree is the repentance of the renouncers (*zohhād*);[1] it is to turn away from an inward desire for the world to having no desire for it.

The third degree is the repentance of the people of presence (*ahl-e hodhur*);[2] it is to turn away from heedlessness to presence.

The fourth degree is the repentance of those who assume traits; it is to turn away from bad moral traits to good moral traits

The fifth degree is the repentance of the gnostics;[3] it is to turn away from seeing one's own good deeds to God. Whenever the people of gnosis attribute a good deed to themselves, they consider repentance from it mandatory; they turn away from their own act to God's act. This is why Rowaim said, "Repentance is to repent of repentance." In other words, if you see repentance — which is a good deed — as deriving from yourself, repent of that repentance and turn to God's relentment, seeing your repentance as an effect of His relentment: "Then He relented toward them that they might repent" (IX:118).

The sixth degree is the repentance of those who profess Divine Unity (*tauḥid*)[4] it is to turn away from everything other than God to God, as was said by Abo'l-Hosain Nuri: "Repentance is that you repent of

1. On renunciation and renouncers, see below, Chapter III, p. 48.

2. For the meaning of 'presence' in sufi terminology, see Nurbakhsh, *Sufism III*, Chapter IV, p. 51-61.

3. On gnosis (*ma'refat* or knowledge) and the gnostics (*'ārefān* or the knowers), see Nurbakhsh, *Sufism [I]: Meaning, Knowledge, and Unity*, Chapter II, p. 43-67.

4. On Divine Unity, see *ibid.*, Chapter III.

everything other than God." Whenever those who profess Divine Unity gaze upon the 'other' (*ghair*), they consider this a sin and regard repenting of this gaze as mandatory. In the midst of this gaze they see that their own existence must be annihilated (*fanā'*)....[1]

In this station, when the existence of the repenter is obliterated and forgotten, how can his sins — which follow upon his existence — remain?

MH 370-371

THE REPENTANCE OF DISCIPLES, SEEKERS, AND REALIZERS

Abu Ya'qub Yusof ebn Ḥamdān Susi said, "The first station of those who cut themselves off from everything but God is repentance." When asked to define it, he said, "Repentance is to turn away from everything which the doctrine (*elm*) blames to that which it praises."

When Sahl ebn 'Abdo'llāh was asked about repentance, he said, "It is that you do not forget your sin."

When Jonaid was asked about repentance, he said, "It is to forget your sin."

This author says: Susi's answer refers to the repentance of disciples, endeavorers, seekers, and strivers, that is, those who sometimes go this way, sometimes that. So also Sahl's answer. But Jonaid's reply — that repentance is to forget one's sin — refers to the repentance of the realizers (*motahaqqequn*). They do not remember their sins because the Grandeur of God and constant

---

1. On 'annihilation', see Nurbakhsh, *Sufism [II]: Fear and Hope...*, Chapter V, p. 85-115.

remembrance of Him has overcome their hearts. Jonaid's answer is similar to that given by Rowaim ebn Aḥmad, when he was asked about repentance: "It is to repent of repentance." Likewise, when Dho'n-Nun was asked about repentance, he replied, "The common people repent of sins, the elect of forgetfulness."

As for the tongue of the gnostics, the finders (*wājedun*), and the elect of the elect concerning repentance, that is what was said by Abo'l-Ḥosain Nuri when he was asked about repentance: "Repentance is that you repent of everything other than God." Dho'n-Nun alluded to this when he said, "The sins of those brought near to God are the good deeds of the pious"; so did the person who said, "The hypocrisy of the gnostics is the sincerity of the disciples." The gnostic was brought near to God by acts of devotion and obedience during the time of his striving, his first beginnings, and his endeavor. When he attained to stability (*tamakkon*) and realized it fully; when the lights of guidance enveloped him, favor came to him, and protection surrounded him; when he witnessed in his heart the Grandeur of his Master which he witnessed; and when he meditated upon the making of his Maker and His ancient beneficence, then he repented of observing, resting in, and attending to the acts of obedience, actions, and devotions which he had performed durring his discipleship and his early stages. What a difference between one repenter and the next! One repenter repents of sins and evil deeds, another of lapses and acts of heedlessness, and a third of seeing good deeds and obedience.

LT 43-44

REPENTANCE OF COMMON PEOPLE, THE ELECT, AND ELECT OF THE ELECT

When the common people repent, they turn away from acts of disobedience; in other words, they ask for forgiveness with the tongue and have remorse in the heart. There is no use in having remorse without asking forgiveness or in asking forgiveness without having remorse. As the Prophet said, "He who asks forgiveness with his tongue but persists in his sin is like one who mocks his Lord."

When the elect repent, they turn away from obedience; in other words, they see their own shortcomings and gaze upon God's kindness. They do not consider any act of obedience worthy of God; they ask pardon for the act in exactly the same way that a disobedient person asks pardon for acts of disobedience.

When the elect of the elect repent, they turn away from creation to God; in other words, they see neither profit nor loss as coming from God's creatures; such a person does not find ease with or depend upon any created thing. He returns from the incapacity, poverty, and meanness of the creatures to the power, riches, and generosity of God.

Hence the reality of repentance is turning away, but the nature of the turning away is diverse.

KST 274

Repentance is remorse at disobedience, such that if the person had the ability to do something similar, he would show no inclination. This is the repentance of the common people. When the elect repent, they leave behind the pleasures of outward form and enter into the private cell of inward meaning.

18

When the elect of the elect repent, they return through volition to the presence of Might, just as death is a return without volition; in the words of the Koran, "Return to thy Lord, well-pleased, well-pleasing!" (LXXXIX:28). In other words: Turn away from substances, accidents, and false goals and return through love to the Threshold of God. Through sincerity, become purified of all sins and defects, so that you may find deliverance and know that 'sin' is everything which veils you from God in this world and the next.

RSh I 185

REPENTANCE OF PENITENCE AND RESPONSE

Dho'n-Nun Meṣri said: "Repentance is of two kinds: The repentance of penitence and the repentance of response (estejābat). Through the 'repentance of penitence' the servant repents in fear of God's punishment, while through the 'repentance of response' he repents in shame before His generosity." Fear is born from the unveiling of God's Majesty, shame from gazing upon His Beauty. In Majesty one servant burns in the fire of fearing Him, while in Beauty another lights up through the light of shame. One is drunk, the other overwhelmed. The people of shame are the companions of intoxication, the people of fear the companions of sobriety.[1]

KM 385

1. For a full disscussion of intoxication and sobriety, see Nurbakhsh, *Sufism [II] Fear and Hope...,* Chapter IV, p. 65-84.

The Koran says, "Repent all together to God"
(XXIV: 31).

> We are sinners,
>> God is Gentle —
> He opened the door to repentance and said,
>> " Come in!"

Repentance means literally 'to return'.

> Whenever something else
>> shows me its face,
> I return from it
>> to His Presence.

The common people return from acts of opposition to
acts of conformity. The Prophet said, "Repentance is
remorse," that is, remorse for any act of obedience or
worship which has slipped by. In the eyes of the jurists
(*foqahā* ') repentance is the greatest pillar.

The renouncers see repentance as remorse for every
missed opportunity to ask forgiveness for sins.

The knowers of God repent through returning to God
from returning to creation.

The gnostics' repentance is: "I seek refuge in Thee
from Thee."[1]

> I return from Him, but to Him —
>> Such is a good return!

The repentance sanctioned by the Shari'at will be
with you only until your last breath. But the repentance

---

1. Reference to the *ḥadith* quoted in note 1, p. 3 above.

Realizers (*mohaqqequn*) will not pass away in this world or the next; it has a beginning, but no end.

> Look at our repentance:
> It has no limit in the two worlds.

Though repentance has been called the 'door of doors,' yet the Prophet, who was forgiven in the text, "That God may forgive thee thy former and thy latter sins" (XLVIII:2), has said, "I ask forgiveness from God seventy times a day."[1]

> Such a repentance
>> has no end.
> It has a beginning,
>> but it knows no limit.

RSh IV 281

CORRECT, MORE CORRECT, AND CORRUPT REPENTANCE

It has been said that repentance is of three kinds: Correct, more correct, and corrupt. In 'correct repentance' the person who sins repents immediately with sincerity, even if he should fall again into sin. The 'more correct' is unswerving repentance. In 'corrupt repentance' he repents with his tongue while the pleasure of disobedience remains in his mind.

KF

---

1. Reference to the *hadith* mentioned in note 1, on page 9 above.

DEFINITIONS OF REPENTANCE BY
THE MASTERS OF THE PATH

The first station of the travelers on the path to God is repentance, just as the first degree of those who seek to do service is purity.... The reality of repentance is to turn away from what God has prohibited toward what is good, as the result of His commandment.

KM 378-79

Repentance is to return to God with continual remorse and much asking of forgiveness after you have gone far from His door by refraining from worship and obedience.

AA 51

Abo'l-'Abbās Sayyāri said, "The tree of knowledge drinks water from the stream of meditation, the tree of heedlessness drinks from the well of ignorance, the tree of repentance drinks from the spring of remorse, and the tree of love drinks from the spring of familiarity and conformity."

MRAn 222

Ebrāhim Adham said, "Repentance is to return toward God with purified consciousness."

TSA 98

Dho'n-Nun Meṣri said, "Every bodily organ must repent. The heart repents by intending to refrain from unlawful passions. The eyes repent by being shut before unlawful sights. The hand repents by refraining from prohibited things. The foot repents by not walking toward prohibited acts. The ears repent by being shut toward vain words. The stomach repents by remaining far from eating unlawful food. The private parts repent by remaining far from indecencies."

TA 222

When Abu 'Ali Rudbāri was asked about repentance, he replied, "Confession, remorse, and abstention."

TSS 366

Imam Ja'far aṣ-Ṣādeq said, "Worship cannot be set right without repentance, for God placed repentance before worship, as in His words, 'The repenters, the worshipers' (IX:112)." The Imam also said, "Remembering repentance during the remembrance of God is to remain heedless of the remembrance."

TA 17

Sahl ebn 'Abdo'llāh said, "The first thing necessary for the beginner is repentance, which is remorse, pulling passions out of the heart, and passing from blameworthy activities to praiseworthy activities. The servant will not find repentance until he clings fast to silence. He will not cling fast to silence until he chooses retreat (khalwat).. Retreat will not come near him until he eats only lawful food (halal). He will not eat only lawful food until he gives God His due. Giving God His due will not be achieved until he guards his bodily parts. And none of these things which we have mentioned will be possible until he asks help from God in all of them."

TA 315

Abu Ḥafṣ Ḥaddād said, "Nothing belongs to the

23

servant in repentance, since repentance comes *to* him, not *from* him."

Abu Bakr Wāseṭi said, "Acceptable repentance is that which was accepted before the sin."

TA 744

Wāseṭi said, "I have no use for a God who would be pleased with me because of my obedience and angry with me because of my disobedience. Then He would be tied to the things I do. No, rather His friends are friends ᵔin eternity without beginning, and His enemies enemies in eternity without beginning."

TA 744

'Abdo'llāh ebn 'Ali ebn Moḥammad at-Tamimi said, "How great is the difference between a repenter who repents of lapses, a repenter who repents of acts of heedlessness, and a repenter who repents of seeing his own good deeds!"

RQ I 321

When Abo'l-Ḥasan Bushanji was asked about repentance, he replied, "When you remember the sin and do not find its sweetness in remembering it, that is repentance."

RQ I 322

Ebrāhim Daqqāq said, "In repentance you are unto God a face without a back, just as before that you had been a back without a face." Turning toward God is the attribute of the face, while turning away from Him is

24

attribute of the back.

Repentance is said to mean turning away from something imperfect and low and going toward something perfect and high.

RA 69

In the early stages repentance is to return and turn away from acts of disobedience, while in the final stages it is to return from the manifestation of the remnants of [your] existence.

RSh IV 170

Repentance is to return to God by untying the knot of persistence from the heart and then performing all one's duties to one's Lord.

TJ

Abu Ḥafṣ Ḥaddād said, "Nothing belongs to the servant in repentance, since repentance comes to him, not from him." God relents toward him, he does not repent toward God. According to this saying, repentance cannot be earned (*moktasab*) by the servant, since it is one of God's gifts. This saying belongs to the school of Jonaid.

KM 385

Abo'l-Ḥasan Bushanji said, "When you remember the sin and find no pleasure in the heart from remembering it, that is repentance." Remembering disobedience is accompanied either by regret or desire. When someone remembers his disobedience with regret and remorse, he is a repenter; but if he remembers disobedience with desire, he is disobedient. The reason for this is that performing the act of disobedience is not nearly as harmful as desiring it, since the act takes place once, but desiring it takes place continually. He who sits with disobedience for an hour in body is not like him who accompanies it night and day in his heart.

KM 385

The root of repentance, which is to turn away from following the *nafs*, is for God's courier to fall into the heart and for the spirit to observe the servanthood (*'obudiyat*) toward its Creator which it has allowed to slip by. The Koran says, "Repent to God with unswerving repentance" (LXVI:8). The Prophet said, "God accepts the servant's repentance as long as he has not breathed his last." Susi was asked about repentance and replied, "Repentance is to turn away from what the doctrine blames to what it praises."

MA 18

REPENTANCE ACCORDING TO ANSARI

The Koran says, "Whosoever does not repent, those — they are the wrongdoers" (XLIX:11), so the name of 'wrongdoing' falls away from the repenter.

There cannot be genuine repentance before true knowledge of sin, which is for you to look at three things in the sin: Your losing [God's] protection by committing it, your pleasure in doing it, and your persistence in not compensating for it — all despite your certainty that God is gazing upon you.

The preconditions for repentance are three: Remorse,

asking pardon, and abstention.

The realities of repentance are three: To acknowledge the misdeed as great, to suspect the repentance, and to seek the pardon of the creatures.

The mysteries of the reality of repentance are three: To discriminate between fear [of God] and [your] reputation, to forget the misdeed, and to repent of repentance forever, for the repenter enters among the 'all' in God's words, "Repent all together to God" (XXIV:31), so He has commanded the repenter to repent.

The subtleties of the mysteries of repentance are three: The first is to confront the misdeed with [God's] decree so that you can come to know God's will in it, for He allowed you to commit it. God only allows the servant to commit sin for one of two reasons:

First, to make known His mightiness in decreeing it, His goodness in concealing it, His clemency in disregarding him who committed it, His generosity in accepting excuses from him, and His bounty in forgiving him.

Second, to set up against the servant the argument for His justice, so that He may punish him for his sin on the basis of the argument.

The second subtlety is for you to know that when the truthful, far-seeing [servant] seeks out his own sin, no good remains with him in that state, for he travels between witnessing kindness and the search for defects in his soul and actions.

The third subtlety is that the servant's witnessing of the decree lets him neither approve good nor disapprove evil, since he ascends beyond all meanings to the meaning of the decree.

The common people repent of making much of obedience, for to do so invites three things: Denying the blessings of [God's] concealment and disregard, thinking that one has claims on God, and self-sufficiency, which is the same as arrogance and presumption before God.

The intermediates repent of making little of disobedience, for to do so is the same as insolence and combat and is nothing but adorning oneself with scorn and abandoning oneself to unfaithfulness.

The elect repent of wasting the present moment (*waqt*), since to do so invites the descending degrees of imperfection, puts out the light of meditation, and muddies the fountain of companionship.

The station of repentance is never completed until it culminates in repentance from everything less than God, then the vision of the deficiency of that repentance, then repentance from the vision of that deficiency.

MS 10-11

The First Field is the station of repentance. Repentance is to return to God. The Koran says: "Repent to God with unswerving repentance" (LXVI:8).

Know that knowledge is life, wisdom a mirror, contentment a fortress, hope an intercessor, remembrance (*dhekr*) a medicine, and repentance a cure-all. Repentance is the mark of the way, the marshall of admittance, the key to the treasure, the intercessor of Union, the go-between of the great, the precondition for acceptance, and the beginning of every happiness.

The pillars of repentance are three: Remorse in the heart, asking pardon with the tongue, and cutting oneself off from bad things and bad people.

28

The kinds of repentance are three: The repentance of the obedient servant, the repentance of the disobedient servant, and the repentance of the gnostic. The obedient servant repents of making much of his obedience. The disobedient servant repents of making little of his disobedience. The gnostic repents of forgetting kindness.

'Making much of obedience' has three signs: Seeing oneself saved through one's own actions, looking upon the purpose of obedience with disdain, and not seeking out the defects of one's own actions.

'Making little of disobedience' has three signs: Considering oneself worthy of forgiveness, being at ease with persistence [in sinning], and being on familiar terms with bad people.

'Forgetting kindness' has three signs: Ceasing to look on oneself with contempt, considering one's own state valuable, and stepping back from the joy of intimacy.

SM 252-53

UNSWERVING REPENTANCE

'Unswerving repentance' is an act performed in the heart. It is to purify the heart of sins. Its sign is that the repenter finds disobedience difficult and ugly, does not return to it, and finds no pleasure in remembering it.

'Unswerving repentance' is to firm up one's determination not to go back to anything similar. Ebn 'Abbās said, "Unswerving repentance is remorse in the heart, asking forgiveness with the tongue, abstention with the body, and resolution not to revert."... It has been said that it leaves no sign of disobedience in the repenter's actions, whether hidden or open; and that it is this repentance which yields deliverance immediately and ultimately."

TJ

Yaḥyā ebn Moʻādh said, "The sign of unswerving repentance is three things: Eating little because of fasting, sleeping little because of prayer, and speaking little because of remembering God."

TA 371

Wāseṭi said, "Unswerving repentance leaves no sign of disobedience in the repenter, whether hidden or open. He whose repentance is unswerving cares not how he sleeps or wakes."

RQ I 321

REPENTING OF REPENTANCE

Since repentance is to manifest one's own existence, and manifesting existence is in the sufi view a great sin, the sufis repent of repentance.

"'Repentance of repentance' is to turn the heart away from everything other than God, even one's own essence and existence. This is annihilation (fanā') in God."

Astonishing creed this Religion of Love!
Repenting of repentance is part of the faith!

MO
30

The way of the annihilated is a different way,
for awareness is a different sin....
You have no knowledge of the Giver of Knowledge,
so your repentance is worse than your sin!
You who repent of your past state —
when, tell me, will you repent of repentance?

M I 2200, 2205-6

Abu Moḥammad Rowaim said, "Repentance is that you repent of repentance." The meaning is what was said by Rābe'a: "I ask forgiveness of God for my lack of truthfulness in my words, 'I ask forgiveness of God'." In other words, the outward asking of God's forgiveness demands truthful dedication in order for it to be a true asking of forgiveness. If such truthful dedication is lacking, the asking of forgiveness becomes another sin, not a repentance. When there is truthfulness of dedication in repentance, the person does not revert. Or the meaning may be that having seen that he relied upon himself in repentance, he repented of this repentance.

KST 275

—II—

ABSTINENCE
wara‘

Abstinence never showed me wine or minstrel—
Love for the Magian youths threw me to both.

Ḥāfeẓ

Abstinence (*wara ʻ*) is to hold oneself back from committing prohibited acts (*manāhi*). It is discussed after repentance because holding oneself back from such acts demands that one first repent. It has been said that abstinence is to avoid doubtful things (*shobohāt*) from fear of falling into unlawful things (*moḥarramāt*).

For friends of God, however, abstinence
is to see with the eye of certainty.

Nāṣer Khosrau

The Prophet said, "The abstainer is he who lets go of the small sin for fear of falling into the great."

KF

35

THE SIGNS OF ABSTINENCE

Yusof ebn Asbāṭ said, "The sign of abstinence is ten things: hesitation in ambiguities, leaving aside doubtful things, scrutiny of food, avoiding distractions, paying heed to more and less, constant contentment with the All-Merciful, accepting trusts with joy, shunning places of harm, remaining distant from the way of maladies, and turning away from pride."

TA 504

THE KINDS OF ABSTINENCE

Ḥabib 'Ajami had a maidservant whose face he did not see for a full thirty years. One day he said to her, "O you with the covered face, call my maidservant!" The maidservant replied, "Am I not your maidservant?" Ḥabib said, "For thirty years I have not had the courage to look at anything without His approval. If my ear does not hear a sound agreeable to religion, it does not listen. If an alien sound reaches it and aims for the heart, the profession of Divine Unity (*tauḥid*) — which is the heart's watchman — does not let it in, but washes the ear with the water of asking forgiveness. In the same way, my tongue keeps watch so that whatever it finds which is not in the way of Truth it does not repeat. My hand keeps watch so as to grasp hold of nothing but the skirt of Reality. My feet keep watch so as to walk on nothing but the ground of His command." Yet, this is still the abstinence of the common people.

As for the abstinence of the elect, that is the abstinence of the heart. If something is not from the

World of Reality, the elect servant does not reflect upon it. If a thought comes to him that is not an influx from God, he sweeps it from the heart's threshold with the broom of repentance and asking forgiveness. When passion throws hopes into the heart, he scours it clean with the hand of trust and fear. When God has not commanded his heart to go someplace, it does not travel there, but makes its home between the two fingers of the All-Merciful.[1]

The difference between outward abstinence and inward abstinence is that when the outward abstainer opens his eyes tomorrow, he will not see God; but the inward abstainer has opened his eyes today and sees God now.

TA II 643

Shebli said, "Abstinence is of three kinds: Abstinence of the tongue, which is to pass over meaningless things in silence and to refrain from meddling; abstinence of the bodily parts, which is to refrain from doubtful things and to avoid 'that which disquiets you for that which does not disquiet you'[2]; and abstinence of the heart, which is to refrain from low aspiration and base thoughts."

MH 372

The people of abstinence are of three classes:
One person among them abstains from doubtful

1. Allusion to the *hadith*, "The hearts of Adam's children are all between two of the All-Merciful's fingers like a single heart that He turns however He desires," found in SMS (*Qadar* 17), ST (*Qadar* 7), and other standard sources.
2. Quotation from the *hadith* that is cited below by Ruzbehān (footnote no. 1, p. 45).

things, that is, all things that lie between the clearly unlawful and the clearly lawful. Everything not called absolutely unlawful or absolutely lawful lies in between, so he abstains from it. Ebn Sirin expressed this position as follows: "There is nothing easier for me than abstinence. When something makes me doubt, I refrain from it."

Another person from among the people of abstinence abstains from that which makes his heart hesitate and which agitates his breast when he takes it. This is known only by the masters of the heart and the realized ones. It is referred to in the Prophet's words, "Sin is that which agitates your breast."[1]

Abu Sa'id Kharrāz said, "Abstinence is that you stay clear of misdeeds toward others, even an atom's weight, so that none of them may stand before you with a misdeed, a claim, or a demand."

In the same way it has been related that Hāreth Mohāsebi never extended his hand toward food about which there was any doubt. Ja'far Kholdi said that he had a vein on the side of his middle finger that would throb if he extended his hand toward doubtful food. Likewise it was related about Beshr Hāfi that he was carried to a reception and food was placed before him. He extended his hand toward it, but his hand would not go forward. He tried again, but again it would not go forward, three times in all. Someone who knew him said, "His hand will not go forward to food which is unlawful or doubtful. The host of this reception

1. The *hadith* is found in SMS (*Berr* 14, 15), ST (*Zohd* 52), and other standard sources in several versions. The text in SMS reads: "Piety (*berr*) is beauty of character, while sin (*ethm*) is that which agitates your breast and about which you hate that people should come to know."

38

gained nothing by inviting this man to his home." This is made stronger by the story of Sahl ebn 'Abdo'llāh. I heard Aḥmad ebn Moḥammad ebn Sālem in Basra saying, "Sahl ebn 'Abdo'llāh was asked about the lawful. He said, 'That in which God has not been disobeyed'." But one can become aware of that in which God has not been disobeyed only through the intimation of the heart.

If someone asks: "Is this attached to a root in the doctrine?" It will be answered: "Yes, the words of the Prophet to Wābesa: 'Ask for a pronouncement from your heart, even if the pronouncers give you a pronouncement.'[1] Also his words, 'Sin is that which agitates your breast.' Do you not see that the Prophet turns the affair over to the heart's intimation?"

The third class in abstinence are the gnostics and the finders (wājedun). Their situation is like what was said by Abu Solaimān Dārāni: "Everything that distracts you from God brings you misfortune;" or by Sahl ebn 'Abdo'llāh when he was asked about the wholly lawful: "The lawful is that in which God is not disobeyed; the wholly lawful is that in which God is not forgotten." Abstinence in which God is not forgotten is that about which Shebli was asked. He answered, "It is that you

1. The versions of this hadith found in standard sources are somewhat different. In SD (Boyu' 2) the text reads: "The Prophet said to Wābesa, 'You have come to ask about piety and sin.' He replied, 'Yes.' Then the Prophet made a fist and struck his chest, saying three times, 'Seek a pronouncement from your own soul, seek a pronouncement from your heart, O Wābesa.' Then he said, 'Piety is that in which your soul gains peace and your heart gains peace; sin is that which agitates the soul and moves back and forth in the breast, even if people give you pronouncements and I give you pronouncements.'"

abstain from letting your heart be dispersed from God for the wink of an eye."

The first is the abstinence of the common people, the second the abstinence of the elect, and the third the abstinence of the elect of the elect.

LT 44-46

SUFI MASTERS' DEFINITIONS OF ABSTINENCE

He is no abstainer, that misguided one,
   who turns his eye toward any but Thee.
To become a stranger to everything other than Thou
   is abstinence, the rest, a tale.

HAu 489

Ebrāhim Adham said, "Abstinence is to refrain from every doubtful thing. And 'to refrain from what is not your own concern'[1] is to refrain from what is superfluous."

RQ I 354

Shebli said, "Abstinence is to abstain from everything other than God."

RQ I 355

Abstinence is to refrain from everything about which there is doubt.

AA 51

1. Reference to the prophetic saying, "Among the good qualities of a man's submission (*eslām*) is that he refrain from what is not his concern" (ST, *Zohd* 11; EM, *Fetan* 12).

Asked about abstinence, Ebrāhim ebn Shaibān replied, "It is for you to remain safe from doubts that upset your breast, and for the Moslems to remain safe, outwardly and inwardly, from the evil of your bodily parts."

TSA 478

There cannot be 'abstinence' from what is prohibited, since abstinence is to refrain from what is doubtful. Some have greatly exaggerated this precaution. They say that abstinence is to refrain from everything, since something may not show its doubtful side outwardly, but still be muddled and mixed; hence one can be fully cautious and safeguard oneself against the thing with certainty by refraining from all things. That is why Jonaid said, "Abstinence is to refrain from everything, for things are mixed."

MH 372

Sahl ebn 'Abdo'llāh said, "Abstinence is the beginning of renunciation, renunciation the beginning of trust (*tawakkol*) trust the beginning of satisfaction (*qanā 'at*), and satisfaction the beginning of contentment (*reḍhā'*)."[1]

MH 373

Yaḥyā ebn Mo'ādh said, "Abstinence is of two kinds: 'Outward abstinence', which means that you move only

---

1. On contentment, see Nurbakhsh, *Sufism III*, Chapter II, p. 11-37.

41

for God; and 'inward abstinence', which means that nothing but God enters your heart."

RQ I 356-57; TA 371

Abu Solaimān Dārāni said, "Abstinence is the beginning of renunciation, just as satisfaction is one side of contentment."

RQ I 356

Yaḥyā ebn Mo'ādh said, "Abstinence is to stop at the limits of the doctrine, without interpretation *(ta'wil)*."

RQ I 356

Sofyān Thauri said, "I have never seen anything easier than abstinence: You refrain from anything that agitates your soul."

RQ I 357

Ebrāhim Khawwāṣ said, "Abstinence is proof of fear *(khauf)*,[1] fear proof of gnosis, and gnosis proof of nearness *(qorbat)*."

MH 373

Beshr Ḥāfi said, "Abstinence is to come out from every doubtful thing and to examine one's soul at every instant."

TA 134

Sahl ebn 'Abdo'llāh said, "Abstinence is to refrain from this world, and this world is the *nafs*.

---

1. On fear and its complement, hope, see Nurbakhsh, *Sufism [II]*, Chapter I, p. 1-27.

takes his own *nafs* as his friend takes God as his enemy."

TA 319

Asked about abstinence, Ebrāhim Khawwāṣ replied, "It is that the servant speaks only the truth, whether he is angry or pleased, and that he strives in that which pleases God."

TSS 284

STATEMENTS OF MASTERS ON ABSTINENCE

Ruzbehān writes:

Once sriritual struggle (*mojāhadat*) has been completed the disciple faces the formalities of abstinence. Its reality is the perfect training of thought after the disappearance of doubts, from which are born egocentric impediments in the region of the heart. This training takes place through the traveler's refraining from those gratifications of human nature that are attained through other than the path of emulation (*iqtidā'*), and through his purifying his inermost consciousness from these gratifications in everything which he undertakes for the sake of his livelihood.

When he reaches perfection in keeping the soul away from the pleasures of nature and when his consciousness achieves detachment through abstaining from attention to other than God, then the brides of the mysteries of Lordship (*robubiyat*) appear to him from behind the curtain of the Unseen in the bridal chambers of Union, the treasury of the lights of the prophetic statutes opens up to his spirit, his heart passes through the confines of the heavens and the earth, and time comes around for

43

him in the guise it had on the day when there was no day, no time, and no space.

Now the sun of favor rises before him and the moon of sufficiency is unveiled. He sees God through God and his yesterday envies his tomorrow, since he has turned his gaze toward sheer eyewitnessing (*'iyān*), averted it from time and space, and entered into the springs of gnosis, whose sources are the oceans of the holiness of witnessing the All-Merciful. He drinks the water of life and then tears the veils of trial. He flies in the air of eternities without beginning, soaring from pre-eternity to eternities without end. He never ceases flying in the stage of the Unseen of the Unseen, beyond all stages. After he reaches stability (*tamkin*)[1] the suns of eternity without beginning rise on him whenever he desires, and he dissolves in their rays just as the moth is consumed by the flame of the candle. When he reaches God through God there remains no more flying, no union, no separation, for when he attains union he subsists (*baqā'*) in God, and when he separates, he is annihilated (*fanā'*) in God.[1] So he sheds both separation and union. The lover and beloved are one in every respect. This is the description of him whose state in unveiling passes beyond the limits of sciences and intellects and whose beginning is the purification of his inmost consciousness through God's addressing him when He says, "O you who have faith, be wary of God with the wariness that is due to Him" (III:102). Among

1. On the meaning of stability, see Nurbakhsh, *Sufism III*, Chapter X, p. 113-124.
2. On annihilation and subsistence, see Nurbakhsh, *Sufism [II]*, Chapter V, p. 85-115.

the Prophet's allusions are his words in teaching courtesy to the gnostic: "Leave that which disquiets you for that which does not disquiet you."[1] Dho'n-Nun said, "The light of gnosis does not extinguish the light of abstinence."

MA 21-22

Anṣāri writes:

The Koran says, "Thy robes purify!" (LXXIV:4).

Abstinence is a deep wariness out of caution, or self-restraint out of acknowledging God's grandeur. It is the last station of renunciation for the common people and the first station of renunciation for the disciple. It has three degrees.

The first degree is to avoid ugly acts, in order to protect the soul, increase beautiful acts, and safeguard faith.

The second degree is to preserve the limits of that to which there is no objection, in order to maintain safeguarding and wariness, ascend from baseness, and be rid of intruding on limits.

The third degree is to abstain from everything that calls you to splinter the present moment and attach yourself to dispersion and from every impediment that blocks the state of gathering (jam ').[2]

MS 24

1. SB, *Boyu'* 3; ST, *Qiāma* 60.

2. On gathering and dispersion, cf. Nurbakhsh, *Sufism [II]*, Chapter III, p. 41-65.

The Fifteenth Field is abstinence. From the Field of Detachment is born abstinence. The Koran says, "If you avoid the great things that are forbidden..." (IV:31). Abstinence is careful avoidance of the blameworthy, of excess, and of unsettled thoughts.

Abstinence from the blameworthy can be had through three things: Keeping oneself away from reproach, keeping one's religion away from decrease, and holding oneself back from greed while walking the path of satisfaction.

Abstinence from excess can be had through three things: The lowliness of the Reckoning, the gloating of enemies, and the fraud of heirs.

Abstinence from unsettled thoughts can be had through three things: Pondering the Koran, visiting cemeteries, and reflection on wisdom.

SM 298-99

زهـد

—III—

RENUNCIATION

zohd

Where's the Minstrel? Let me take everything
    I've gained through renunciation and knowledge
and put them to work for the
    lute's strumming and the reed's call.

Ḥāfeẓ

Renunciation is to turn the heart's inclination away
from something lower and toward something higher. At
the beginning renunciation is to refrain from this world,
during the middle stages it is to refrain from both this
world and the next through seeking God, and at the end
it is to abandon one's own existence in love for God.
The station of renunciation comes after repentance and
abstinence.

"'Ali said, "Renunciation is that you do not care who eats of this world, faithful or unbeliever." 'Ali was speaking about his own situation, since his family had no more food than was absolutely necessary and they had need of that food, yet for the sake and love of God they gave it to the needy, the orphan, and the prisoner. Then God praised them with the words, "They give food, for the love of Him, to the needy, the orphan, the prisoner" (LXXVI:8). And this prisoner was an unbeliever. If refraining from this world for an unbeliever were not renunciation, God's praise would not have been deemed necessary, since the good is praised, not the evil."

KST 277-78

THE SIGNS OF RENUNCIATION

Aḥmad Anṭāki said, "The signs of renunciation are four: Reliance upon God, aversion toward creation, sincerity toward God, and putting up with injustice to preserve the honor of religion."

TA 411

DIFFERENCE BETWEEN SUFI AND RENOUNCER

Abu 'Abdo'lāh Torughbadi was asked, "Who is the sufi and who the renouncer?"

He replied, "The sufi is [so] through his Lord, the renouncer through himself."

TA 557; TSA 550

50

DIFFERENCE BETWEEN
RENOUNCER AND GNOSTIC

Naṣrābādi said, "The renouncer is a stranger in this world, the gnostic a stranger in the next world."

Yahyā ebn Mo'ādh said, "The renouncer makes you sniff vinegar and mustard, the gnostic lets you smell musk and ambergris."

EO IV.4.2 (171)

RENUNCIATION OF THE GNOSTIC
AND THE NON-GNOSTIC

For other than the gnostic, renunciation is a transaction. It as as if he buys the goods of the next world with the goods of this world. For the gnostic it is to be far above everything that distracts from God and to be haughty toward everything other than God.

RSh I 135

RENOUNCER AND THE PSEUDO-RENOUNCER

Shaqiq Balkhi said, "The renouncer is he who renounces with his acts, the pseudo-renouncer he who renounces with his tongue."

TSS 57

THE RENOUNCERS AND THE GREAT-HEARTED

Mohammad ebn Fadhl said, "When the renouncers have no need, they show preference for others; the great-hearted show preference for others when they themselves have need. The Koran says, 'They prefer

51

others above thenselves, even though privation be their portion' (LIX:9)."

THE KINDS OF RENUNCIATION

Imam Ahmad ebn Ḥanbal said, "Renunciation is of three sorts: First, refraining from what is unlawful, this being the renunciation of the common people. Second, refraining from the lawful that is superfluous, this being the renunciation of the elect. Third, refraining from what distracts the servant from God, this being the renunciation of the gnostics."

RQ I 372-73; TA 261

Sahl ebn 'Abdo'llah said, "Three things are renounced: First, clothing, for it will end up in the garbage pit. Second, brothers, for that will end in separation. Third, this world, for it will end up in annihilation."

TA 319

THE LEVELS OF RENUNCIATION

We consider renunciation to consist of three levels: The first level, renunciation of this world, is of three kinds. The first kind is that a person refrains outwardly while inclining inwardly; he is called a pseudo-renouncer and is the object of God's hate.[1] The second kind is that he refrains outwardly and inwardly, but he is aware of his refraining and knows that he is a refrainer; we consider him imperfect. The third kind is that he gives

1. Allusion to the Koranic verse, "Very hateful is it to God that you saywhat you do not do."(LXI:3)

no importance or value to refraining, so that he does not know that he is refraining from anything; we consider him perfect in refraining from this world. However, he refrains for the sake of the next world and its bliss.

The second level is that of the person who refrains from both this world and the next, but he does not refrain from his own self. In other words, he wants the Lord for the sake of himself, so his wanting is for his own self. This is also the level of someone who is perfect but unripe.

The third level is that of the person who refrains from this world, the next world, and his own selfhood. In other words, his gaze is totally upon the Lord. He has forgotten himself and other than himself and has given the whole of himself to the Lord. He does not want himself except for His sake and is unaware of wanting and not wanting. We call him the most perfect in perfection.

KF 612

THE KINDS OF RENOUNCERS

There are three classes of renouncers: First, the beginners, who empty their hands of possessions and their hearts of what has left their hands. Thus Jonaid was asked about renunciation and he replied, "Emptying the hands of possessions and emptying the heart of desire." When Sari Saqati was asked about renunciation, he answered, "It is that his heart be empty of that of which his hands are empty."

Another group have fully realized renunciation. Their description is given in Rowaim's answer to a question about renunciation: "Refraining from everything in this

53

world that gratifies the soul." This is the renunciation of those who have attained full realization, for the soul finds gratification in renouncing this world, since renunciation brings about ease and the praise, commendation, and respect of the people. So he whose heart renounces all these gratifications has fully realized renunciation.

The third group know and have certainty that if all of this world were their lawful possession, for which they will not be called to account in the next world and which will not detract anything from what God has for them, and if they were to renounce it for God's sake, they would have renounced something which God has not looked upon since creating it. If this world weighed a gnat's wing in God's eyes, He would not have given an unbeliever to drink of its water. So they renounce their renunciation and repent of it. When Shebli was asked about renunciation, he replied, "Renunciation is heedlessness, since this world is nothing, and renouncing nothing is heedlessness." Yahyā ebn Mo'ādh said, "This world is like a bride. He who seeks it is her hairdresser. He who renounces it blackens her face, plucks out her hair, and tears her clothing. But the gnostic is busy with God and pays no attention to it."

LT 46-47

DEFINITIONS OF RENUNCIATION BY MASTERS OF THE PATH

Yahyā ebn Mo'ādh said, "Renunciation (*zohd*) is made up of three letters, *z*, *h*, and *d*. *Z* is to refrain from fancy clothing (*zinat*), *h* is to refrain from caprice (*hawā*), and *d* is to refrain from this world (*donyā*)."

TA 371

Ḥallāj said, "Refraining from this world is the renunciation of the soul, refraining from the next world the renunciation of the heart, and refraining from self the renunciation of the spirit."

TA 589

Dho'n-Nun Meṣri said, "Certainty invites to having few hopes, having few hopes invites to renunciation, renunciation invites to wisdom, and wisdom yields looking at ultimate ends."

TA 155

When asked about renunciation, Bāyazid replied, "Renunciation has no value. I renounced for three days: On the first this world, on the second the next world, and on the third everything but God."

TA 197

'Abdo'llāh ebn Mobārak said, "Renunciation is to be confident in God and to love poverty."

TA 219; RQ I 369

Ḥamdun Qaṣṣār was asked about renunciation and replied, "In my view it is that your heart does not feel more secure with what is in your hand than with what is vouched for by God."

TA 404

Abu 'Othmān Ḥiri said, "Renunciation is to wash one's hands of this world and not to care in whose hands it might be."

TA 480

Abu Mohammad Rowaim said, "Renunciation is to look down on this world and to obliterate its traces from the heart."

TA 486

Abu 'Abdo'llāh Mohammad ebn Khafif said, "Renunciation is to find ease in abandoning possessions."

TA 578; RQ I 368

Asked about renunciation, Shebli replied, "It is nothing. That which will be yours must reach you, even if you flee from it. And that which will not be yours will never reach you, even if you seek and strive and struggle. So what will you renounce? That which will be yours, or that which will not be yours?"

TA 633

Asked on another occasion about renunciation, Shebli replied, "It is to turn the heart toward the Creator of all things."

TA 633

When Abo'l-'Abbās Qaṣṣāb was asked about renunciation, he replied, "I was standing on the shore of the Ocean of the Unseen with a shovel in my hand. I dug in the shovel and with the first scoop lifted up everything from God's Throne down to the earth, so there was nothing left for the second scoop. This is the lowest degree of renunciation." In other words, in the first step every form disappeared from his view.

TA 644

Abu Bakr Wāseṭi, "Those people of renunciation who are proud before the children of this world are pretenders to renunciation. If this world did not display some sparkle to their hearts, they would not be proud before others for turning away from it." He also said, "Why do you bring such force to bear in renouncing and turning away from something, when the whole of it is not worth a gnat's wing in God's eyes?"

TA 745

Abo'l-Ḥasan Ḥoṣri said, "I asked someone about renunciation and he replied, 'It is to leave that in which you are for him who is in it.'"

TA 761; RQ I 371

Abu Solaimān Dārāni said, "The sign of renunciation is that if someone should let you wear a woolen frock whose price is three dirhams, no desire falls into your heart for a frock whose price is five dirhams.'

TA 280

Ḥātem Aṣamm said, "The beginning of renunciation is reliance upon God, its middle patience, and its end sincerity."

TA 302

Yahyā ebn Mo'ādh said, "Renunciation gives rise to

generosity with possessions, while love gives rise to generosity with soul and spirit."

TA 371

Yahyā ebn Mo'ādh said, "Renunciation means that a person is greedier in refraining from this world than in seeking it."

TA 371

Yahyā ebn Mo'ādh said, "The renouncer is outwardly pure but inwardly mixed, while the gnostic is inwardly pure but outwardly mixed."

TA 371

Yusof ebn Hosain said, "A sign of renunciation is that the person does not seek what is lost until he loses what he has found."

TA 388

Some say that renunciation is of the unlawful...; others say that renunciation of the unlawful is mandatory, and of the lawful a virtue.

RQ I 365-66

Sofyān Thauri said, "Renunciation in this world is to have no expectations. It is not that you eat coarse food or wear a cloak."

RQ I 367

Some of them say that the servant must not choose to refrain from what is lawful such that he burdens himself,

58

nor must he choose to seek for more than he needs. He must observe his allotted portion. If God provides him lawful possessions, he should thank Him, and if He keeps him at the limit of sufficiency, he should not burden himself by seeking possessions that are superfluous. Patience is best for the poor man, while thanksgiving is more suited for him who has lawful possessions.

RQ I 366

Ebn Masruq said, "The renouncer is he who is not owned by any secondary cause, only by God."

T 93

Abu Soliamān Dārāni said, "Renunciation is to refrain from everything that distracts from God."

RQ I 369

Yaḥyā ebn Mo'ādh said, "No one reaches the reality of renunciation until three traits are found within him: Actions without attachment, words without desire, might without leadership."

RQ I 370

'Amr ebn 'Othmān Makki said, "Know that the head and root of renunciation in hearts is contempt for this world, deeming it of little significance, and looking upon it with an eye that sees paltriness. This is the root from which grows the reality of renunciation."

TSS 196

Ebrāhim Adham said, "Renunciation of the unlawful

is mandatory. It is a virtue to refrain from the lawful if there is more than necessary. Renunciation by refraining from doubtful things is a noble trait, since refraining from doubtful things gives rise to noble-mindedness."

KF 610

Sari Saqati said, "Renunciation is to refrain from all the gratifications of the *nafs* found in this world. The renouncer does not become happy through anything within this world, nor does he become sad at losing anything of it. He takes nothing from it except that which helps him obey his Lord or that which he is commanded to take, while he occupies himself continually with remembrance, meditation, and reflection about the next world. This is the highest state of renunciation. When someone reaches this degree, his person is in this world, but his spiritual reality is with God through meditation and witnessing, and he does not become separate from God."

KF 610

When asked about renunciation, Moḥammad ebn Faḍhl Balkhi replied, "To look upon this world with the eye that sees imperfections, and to live with honor and respect while turning away from this world."

NO 117

Renunciation is to refrain from all the lawful things of this world and to turn away from this world and its passions.

AA 51

Jonaid said, "Renunciation is that the hands be empty

60

of possessions and the heart of pursuit." The reason that the servant must be empty of possessions is that he himself is an owned slave, and a slave cannot have possessions. Pursuit is craving, while renunciation is the opposite of craving, and opposites cannot coincide. The reality of renunciation is to detach the heart, not to empty the hand. So if the servant should achieve both, that is the perfection of the station of renunciation.

KST 277

Yaḥyā ebn Mo'ādh said, "Renunciation is to refrain from the cure." 'The cure' is that from which the servant cannot flee. For example, if a person should be niggardly to the extent of curing [a predicament], to that very extent he has relied upon other than God. If God wants, He will take care of him without that cure, and he will know that God takes care of him, not the cure. For the gnostics, 'that from which one has no cure' is God, since without anything, things can be accomplished, but without God, nothing can be accomplished.

KST 278

A great man was traveling in the desert without provisions. Someone said, "Where are your provisions?" He answered, "My provisions are that I have no cure against Him who has a cure for me." In other words: I have no need for food, since food was created for me, but I have need for God, while God has no need for me. I seek Him for whom I have need, while food, which has need for me, itself seeks me.

KST 278

Shāh Ne'mato'llāh writes:

The forbearing renouncer must come out of the private cell of bodily pleasure and renounce the goods of this world and egocentric enjoyment, whether little or much, possessions or position, friends or strangers, just as a person becomes wearied of all things through compulsory death.[1]

The reality of renunciation is that you renounce through the will this world and the next, just as the Manifestation of Guidance and Grace [the Prophet] has said: "This world is unlawful to the people of the next world, the next world is unlawful to the people of this world, and both are unlawful to the people of God."

> This world and the next are
> the caravansaries of the common people,
> but we have fastened the lock of aversion
> on the doors of both inns.

RSh I 186

Ruzbehān writes:

Renunciation of everything less than God is the sufi's watchword. He begins his covenant by coming outside the *nafs*, passion, this world, the next world, and everything within them and taking up his dwelling at the station of affliction (*balā'*).

He travels on the steed of intimacy to the world of holiness, until he sees from God that which will never be perceived by the people of rational understanding

---

1. In other words, physical death, as opposed to the 'voluntary death' to the *nafs* chosen by the sufis.

through their intellectual abstrusities based on truthful and incontrovertible proofs concerning the necessities of argument and their speculation on the priority of Eternity. After cutting off formalities and the signs of the speculative thinkers, he attains to the intimacy of the shining of sempiternity's flashes.

After the rising of the sun of nearness, he settles in his inmost consciousness into his first, holy, primordial nature. Through the light of his primordial nature he witnesses the light of the Attributes and falls in love with the beauty of the Essence. He frees his neck from the bondage of time and the pattern of space. The affectations of the natural world, such as renunciation and dedication to actions, fall away from him, and he is granted the robe of election and distinction. He witnesses God in the world without the world.

In the same way God commanded His beloved Moḥammad to shut his eyes toward the kingdom of existence, and He described his eyes as being far above swerving toward anything less than He. In the first case He said, "Let not thine eyes turn away [from them, desiring the adornment of the life of this world]" (XVIII:28), and in the second He said, "His eye swerved not" (LIII:17). The Prophet said, "What do I have to do with this world?" The gnostic says, "Renunciation is to lift the gaze beyond everything less than the Friend."

MA 22

Anṣārī writes:
The Koran says, "What remains with God is better for you" (XI:86). Renunciation is totally to eliminate

63

desire for things. For the common people it is a devotion, for the disciple a necessity, and for the elect an act of meanness. It has three degrees:

The first degree is renunciation of the doubtful — after refraining from the unlawful — by being cautious of the blameworthy, scorning imperfection, and detesting association with the ungodly.

The second degree is renunciation of the superfluous and all food beyond that which supports and suffices, by seizing the opportunity of idleness to cultivate the present moment, settle agitation, and become adorned with the adornment of the prophets and the righteous.

The third degree is renunciation of renunciation through three things: Disdaining what you have renounced, seeing all states as equivalent, and going beyond the sight of acquisition by gazing upon the valley of realities.

MS 23-24

The Thirteenth Field is renunciation. From the Field of Wakefulness is born renunciation. The Koran says, "What remains with God is better for you" (XI:86). Renunciation is of three things: This world, people, oneself. Whoever does not begrudge his enemy the good fortune of this world has renounced this world. Whoever is not made into a hypocrite toward God by respect for people has renounced people. Whoever does not look upon himself with the eye of approval has renounced himself.

The sign of renunciation of this world is three things: Remembering death, satisfaction with food, companionship with darvishes.

64

The sign of renunciation of the creatures is three things: Seeing the precedence of God's decree, the correctness of destiny, and the impotence of the creatures.

The sign of renunciation of self is three things: Recognizing the guile of the devil, the frailty of one's self, and the darkness of being led on little by little.[1]

SM 295-96

1. Allusion to such Koranic verses as, "And those who cry lies to Our signs, We shall lead them on little by little, whence they know not" (VII:182).

—IV—

WARINESS

taqwā

Not I alone fell
from the retreat of wariness —
My father let everlasting paradise
slip from his hand.

Ḥāfeẓ

Literally, *taqwā* ("wariness") signifies to be on one's guard. In sufi terminology, it means to be on one's guard against everything other than God.

'Ali said, "The lords of men in this world are the generous, the lords of men in the next world the wary."

RQ I 351

THE ROOT OF WARINESS

Taqwā has two root meanings: First, 'to fear', and second, 'to be on one's guard'. The servant's wariness toward God also has two meanings: Either fear of punishment, or fear of separation. The sign of the fear of punishment is that, in order not to merit punishment, the

69

servant never opposes the statutes of God's commandments and prohibitions, while he maintains the rights and the limits of companionship. As for the fear of separation, in order not to be apart from God he stays on his guard against everything less than God and does not find ease with other than Him.

KST 294

THE PRECONDITION OF WARINESS

The first precondition of wariness is that you be the watchman of your own heart and accomplish three things: Never let yourself feel secure, be on your guard against everything blameworthy, and do not forget God for a single instant.

TFA 539

THE KINDS OF WARINESS

There are three kinds of wariness: Being on one's guard against associating anything with God (*sherk*), which is the wariness of the common people; being on one's guard against sin, which is the wariness of the elect; and being on one's guard against doubt, which is the wariness of the elect of the elect.

TFA I 178

It has been said that there are a number of kinds of wariness: That of the common people is to be wary of associating anything with God, that of the elect is to be wary of acts of disobedience, that of God's friends is to be wary of seeking access [to God] through acts, and

70

that of the prophets is to be wary of attributing acts [to oneself], since they are wary of Him through Him.[1]

RQ I 351

THE SIGN OF WARINESS

Shāh Kermāni said, "The sign of wariness is abstinence, and the sign of abstinence is to refrain from doubtful things."

TA 380

OUTWARD AND INWARD ASPECT OF WARINESS

Ebn 'Atā' said, "Wariness has an outward and an inward aspect. Its outward aspect is observing rights and limits, its inward, intention and sincerity."

TA 495

BĀYAZID'S WARINESS

In Hamadān Bāyazid bought some safflower seeds, and a few were left over. When he returned to Bastām he found two ants in the seeds. So he returned to Hamadān and left the ants.

Once Bāyazid was washing his clothes in the wastelands with a companion. The companion said, "Hang the clothes on the wall of the vineyard." Bāyazid replied , "No, do not stick pegs into people's walls." He said, "Let us hang them on the tree." Bāyazid replied, "No, that will break the branches." He said, "Let us spread them on the plants." He replied, "No, that is

---

1. Allusion to the *hadith* mentioned above: "I take refuge in Thee from Thee."

food of the livestock, so we should not cover them." So he placed the shirt on his back and turned it toward the sun, until one side of it dried. Then he turned it over and dried the other side.

One day Bāyazid entered a mosque. He planted his staff in the ground, but it fell over onto the staff of an old man, who had fixed his staff in the ground, and knocked it down. The old man bent over and picked up his staff. Afterwards Bāyazid went to the house of the old man and asked his pardon, saying, "The reason you bent over was my negligence in planting my staff, so it then became necessary for you to bend over."

RQ I 349-50

WARINESS DEFINED BY MASTERS OF THE PATH

Mohammad ebn Sanjān said, "Wariness is to refrain from everything less than God." This does not mean that a person should know nothing but God, since the prophets are other than God, and until a person has faith in the prophets, he cannot be wary. Rather, it means that he should eliminate all desire and dread toward anything other than God; for whenever the servant becomes a thing's companion, he does so either with desire or with dread. When both are removed, he has refrained from created existence, and when he refrains from everything other than God, that is true wariness.

KST 295-96

One of the sufis said, "The root of wariness is to avoid the prohibited and keep apart from the *nafs*. To the extent the servant passes beyond the gratifications of the *nafs*, he reaches certainty."

T 99

Sahl ebn 'Abdo'llāh said, "Wariness is to witness states in the measure of keeping apart." This means that everything which makes the servant inwardly happy causes him to incline toward itself and to rest in it. To the extent that he inclines toward other than God, he turns away from God and remains apart from Him. The 'states' of the servant are either outward states, such as obedience, or inward states, such as witnessing, hope, fear, and the like. Sahl says: The servant must keep apart from these states. Then he will be wary not in the sense of avoiding disobedience and ungodliness, but in the sense of doing everything completely, without seeing the act as something he has done himself. Since he always sees himself as falling short, he never rests and always seeks better from himself, just as the Koran has said: "Be wary toward God to the extent you are able" (LXIV:16), that is, to the extent of your full capacity. So wariness means that no matter what your state may be, you look toward God, not toward the state, and you rest in nothing less than God.

KST 294-95

Literally *taqwā* means to be on one's guard and to fear God, while in sufi terminology it means to be on one's guard against everything other than God, to refrain from all sins, and to stay far from this world and its concomitants.[1]

1. Cf. RQ I 344 ff.

Naṣrābādi said, "Wariness is for the servant to be wary of everything other than God."

RQ I 346

Dho'n-Nun said, "The wary one is he who does not soil his outward being with acts of resistance or his inward with diversions. He stands with God in the station of harmony."

RQ I 347

Wāseṭi said, "Wariness is to be wary of one's wariness," that is to be wary of seeing one's own wariness.

RQ I 348

Wariness comprehends all good qualities. Its reality is to be on one's guard against God's punishment by obeying Him. Thus it is said, "So-and-so was wary with his shield." The root of wariness is to be wary of associating anything with God, then of acts of disobedience and evil deeds, then of doubtful things; finally it is to put aside everything superfluous.

RQ I 345

Ḥariri said, "Whoever fails to allow wariness and meditation to govern between him and God will never reach unveiling and witnessing."

RQ I 346

It has been said, "Three things point to a man's wariness: Perfect trust in that which he has not attained, perfect contentment in that which he has already attained, and perfect patience in that which has slipped by."

RQ I 348

Abu 'Abdo'llāh Khafif said, "Wariness is to stay far away from everything that keeps you far from God."

TA 578

Shaqiq Balkhi said, "Wariness can be known by three things: Sending, holding back, and speaking. 'Sending' is religion," that is, that which you send there [to God] is religion; "'holding back' is this world," that is, you do not take the possessions which you are given, since they belong to this world; "and 'speaking' is in both religion and this world," that is, one can speak about both abodes, since there are words about religion and words about this world. Another meaning is that what you send is religion, that is, carrying out God's commandments; holding back is this world, that is, remaining far from what He has prohibited; speaking encompasses both, since speaking makes clear whether a man is in religion or this world.

TA 238

Ebn Jalā' said, "Wariness is thanksgiving for knowledge, humility thanksgiving for high standing, and patience thanksgiving for affliction."

TA 498

Abu Moḥammad Rāsebi said, "Whenever the servant's heart is tested by wariness, love for this world and love for passions are removed from it, and it is conscious of unseen things."

TSA 561

Nahrajuri said, "This world is the ocean, the next world the shore, wariness the boat, and people the travelers. Travelers have no escape from boat and provisions."

RAS 196

The root of wariness is to disengage the inmost consciousness — through gazing upon the witnesses of the Attributes and the flashes of the Essence — from attending to impediments deriving from both the corporeal realm *(molk)* and the spiritual realm *(malakut)*; one melts away in recognizing the majesty of the unveilings of the brilliance of Eternity's assaults. To this alludes the Prophet's words, "Faith is naked, its clothing wariness." The gnostic says, "Wariness is the gauge of the hearts of the gnostics and the manifestation of the inmost consciousness of the righteous."

MA 30

ANṢĀRI'S WORDS ON WARINESS

The Sixteenth Field is wariness. Wariness is born out of abstinence. The Koran says, "Whoever is wary, and is patient..." (XII:90); "And of Me be wary!" (II:41). The wary are three men: The small, the middle, and the great.

The small is he who does not mix his profession of Divine Unity *(tauhid)* with associating others with God *(sherk)*, his sincerity with hypocrisy, or his worship with innovation *(bed 'at)*.

76

The middle is he who does not mix his companionship with false show, his food with the doubtful, or his state with neglect.

The large is he who does not mix blessings with complaint or his own fault with argument, nor does he ever rest upon seeing God's kindness toward himself.

SM 299-300

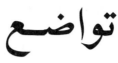

—V—

HUMILITY

tawāḍhoʻ

If the eminent show humility,
    that's fine.
If a beggar shows humility,
    that's his nature.

Sa'di

Humility (*tawādho'*) is to see oneself as less than others and to respect God's creatures. In sufi terminology it means that you see everything which comes to you as coming from God, so you submit to Him and do not protest His decree.

THE ROOT OF HUMILITY

Abu 'Othmān Ḥiri said, "The root of humility lies in the servant's remembering three things: His ignorance, his sin, and his need for God."

TA 481

81

THE SIGN OF HUMILITY

Yusof Asbāṭ said, "The sign of humility is that you accept true words, no matter who may have spoken them."

TA 503

THE EXTREME LIMIT OF HUMILITY

Shebli said, "I asked Yusof Asbāṭ about the extreme limit of humility. He replied, 'When you come out of your house, you consider everyone you see better than yourself.'"

TA 503

THE MOST USEFUL HUMILITY

Aḥmed ebn 'Āṣem Anṭāki said, "The most useful humility is that which expels your pride and quenches your wrath."

TSS 128

EXAMPLES OF HUMILITY FROM GREAT SUFIS

I have heard that on a feast-day,
in the morning, early,
out from the bathhouse
came the great Bāyazid.
Without any warning
down from a window
a pail full of ashes
was thrown on his head.

82

His turban blackened,
his beard filthied,
he stroked his face
in gratitude:
"My soul,
I am worthy of the Fire.
Should I then become angry
at a pail full of ashes?"
The great never look
at themselves —
Seek not the vision of God
from self-seers!

B 116

I have heard that Jonaid saw a dog
    in Ṣanʿā desert,
its teeth fallen out,
    unable to hunt.
Its claws had once had the power
    to seize great lions,
but now it was broken,
    a decrepit old fox.
Once it ran after
    wild goat and antelope,
now it ate the kicks
    of the bedouin's sheep.
Seeing it wretched,
    helpless and wounded,
Jonaid gave it half

of his own provisions.
Weeping and wailing,
    he said — so I've heard —
"Who knows which is the better
    of the two of us here?
Today it may seem that
    I have the honor,
but what will destiny
    bring down on my head?"

B 132

Once the Water-carrier
    who fills the Nile
held back Egypt's water
    for the length of a year.
A group went off
    to the mountains,
pleading and praying
    that He might send down the rain.
They wept,
    and their weeping
brought a stream,
    but not a drop of heaven's tears.
One of them took the news
    to Dho'n-Nun:
"The people are suffering,
    overcome by great pain.
Say a prayer
    for the helpless —

he whom God accepts
      will not be repulsed."
Dho'n-Nun then fled
      to Midian
and before long
      the rain came down.
After twenty days
      in Midian he heard
that a black-hearted cloud
      had wept over Egypt.
Relieved,
      the shaykh came back
for the river was full
      with the flood of Spring.
A gnostic then asked him
      all in secret,
"Why in fact
      did you go from here?"
He said, "I have heard that the birds,
      the ants and the beasts
want for provisions
      because of evil men's deeds.
I thought deeply
      about this land
and saw none more distracted
      than me myself.
So I went,
      lest my evil
shut the door of good

to everyone here."

B 134-135

HUMILITY DEFINED BY MASTERS OF THE PATH

Fodhail ebn 'Eyādh said, "Whoever sees himself as having worth has no share in humility."

RQ I 432

Asked about humility, Fodhail ebn 'Eyādh replied, "You submit to the truth, follow it, and accept it from anyone who utters it."

RQ I 434

It has been said, "Humility is being proud with little, embracing lowliness, and taking on the burdens of the people of religion."

T 97

'Abdo'llāh ebn Mobārak said, "Being proud before the rich and humble before the poor is part of humility."

RQ I 433

Bāyazid was asked, "When does a man have humility?" He replied, "When he sees himself as possessing neither station nor state and sees no one among God's creatures worse than himself."

RQ I 433

It has been said, "Humility is a blessing which no one envies, while pride is a trial toward which no mercy is shown. High standing lies in humility. He who searches for it in pride will not find it."

Yahyā ebn Mo'ādh said, "Humility is beautiful in everyone, but more beautiful in the rich. Pride is ugly in everyone, but uglier in the poor."

RQ I 434

Ebn 'Aṭā' said, "Humility is to accept the truth from whomsoever it may come."

RQ I 434

'Abdo'llāh Rāzi said, "Humility is to refrain from making distinctions in rendering service."

RQ I 435

Ḥamdun Qaṣṣār said, "Humility is that you see no one in need of you — whether in religion or in worldly affairs — in this world or the next."

RQ I 438

Abu Solaimān Dārāni said, "Humility is that you never admire yourself for your own actions."

TA 280

Dārāni said, "The servant will not have humility until he ceases knowing himself."

TA 280

87

Yaḥyā ebn Moʿādh said, "The highest forbearance is humility."

TA 370

Ḥamdun Qaṣṣār said, "The true position of the darvish lies in the extent of his humility. If he refrains from humility, he has refrained from all good."

TA 403

Abu ʿAli Daqqāq said, "The humility of the rich is the religion of the poor, while the humility of the poor is the treachery of the rich."

TA 655

Jonaid was asked about humility. He replied: "Lowering the wing and breaking the side." In other words, it is to be soft, obedient, loving, and long-suffering. Humility toward God is to obey His commands, not to protest against His acts, and to be pleased with everything He does.

KST 289

Rowaim said, "Humility is the lowliness of hearts before the Knower of Unseen Things." In other words, what can the servant do but be lowly, poor, and impotent before his Lord?

KST 289

Sahl ebn ʿAbdoʾllāh said, "The perfection of God's remembrance is witnessing, while the perfection of

humility is to be content with Him" and with everything
He does, and not to want anything from God but God.

KST 289

A great one said, "Humility is accepting the truth
from the Truth for the sake of the Truth." In other
words, you should conform yourself to God and be as
you should toward Him in whatever comes your way.

KST 289

Yusof ebn Ḥosain Rāzi said, "Good is all in a single
house whose key is humility, and evil is all in a single
house whose key is pride."

TSA 268

Mozaffar Kermānshāhi said, "Humility is to accept
the truth from him who has it."

TSA 485

Ruzbehān said, "Humility springs from humbleness:
The servant is annihilated in God's Grandeur and made
lowly by His Magnificence in the vision of what can be
seen of the witnesses of His Singularity and Oneness,
until he reaches God with the attribute of annihilation
and subsists in His Subsistence. The Prophet said, 'He
who has humility is raised up by God.'"

MA 31

In the early stages humility is outward and for sake of
religion, but in the final stages it is the return to one's
original nonexistence in God's Being.

RSh IV 175

THE STATION OF THE BELOVED'S HUMILITY
IN THE LOVER

This is one of the stations of obscurity and the attributes of ambiguity. It occurs when the lover has attained stability in the profession of Divine Unity and gnosis, and God wants to honor him and acknowledge his greatness so that he will be great among the creatures through God's Greatness and will know himself in the place of Magnificence. The gnostic says, "This is a reality, but it is a deception in order to delight the lover's heart."

MA 289

STATEMENTS OF THE GREAT MASTERS
CONCERNING HUMILITY

'Ezzo'd-Din Kāshāni writes:

Humility is to place oneself with God in the station of servanthood (ʿbudiyat) and with God's creatures in the station of just treatment (enṣāf)

'Placing oneself with God in the station of servanthood' takes place when one first follows His commands and prohibitions, second receives the theophanies of His Attributes, or third experiences the annihilation of one's existence in the theophany of the Essence. Following commands and prohibitions in the soul is the humility of beginners. Reception of the theophanies of the Attributes in the heart along with the annihilation of one's own will in the Will of God is the humility of the intermediates. Reception of the theophany of the Essence in the spirit with the annihilation of one's own existence in Absolute Being is

90

the humility of those at the end of the path.

What is meant by 'placing oneself with God's creatures in the station of just treatment' is either the acceptance of the truth or observing rights while refraining from elevation or expectation. By 'acceptance of truth' is meant that whenever a person witnesses the truth from the other side during debates and disputes, he never follows the road of obstinacy, but comes forward in fairness and submission. Though outwardly he has shown humility to creatures in this situation, inwardly he has shown humility toward the Truth. That is why Fodhail 'Eyādh said, "Humility is that you lower yourself before the truth, follow it, and accept it from anyone who utters it and anyone from whom you hear it." The following sound hadith alludes to the same meaning: "God has revealed to me that you should have humility...and that some of you should not oppress others."[1]

By 'observing rights' is meant that the person should not trample over the rights of others but rather consider them to have priority over his own rights....

By 'refraining from elevation or expectation' is meant that he does not enter among people at a level above what he deserves; on the contrary, he does not expect people to observe the right of his own level.

The reality of humility is to observe the equilibrium between pride and deprecation. Pride is to conceive of the self at a higher and more elevated level than it deserves.

Deprecation is to neglect its right and to place it in a level below its right. To observe and maintain the

1. SMS, *Janna* 64. Also SD (*Adab* 40) and EM (*Zohd* 16, 23).

measure of equilibrium is an extremely rare station. Feet slip in trying to conceive of it, since as long as the traces of existence and its attributes remain in the soul, it tends toward pride and evaluates itself at a level beyond what it merits. Therefore, when the masters of the path saw this illness hidden in the soul, they set out to cure it and to expel it by directing most of their sayings about humility toward deprecation. Were it not for the fact that defiance of the measure of equilibrium and inclination toward pride is kneaded into the soul, and were the soul not in need of a cure and content with its own waystation, the masters would not have turned the disciples toward deprecation.

In the early stages of the manifestation of the power of state (*ḥāl*), few travelers are empty of the quehcning and satiety which give rise to intoxication; by the fact of eavesdropping[1] their souls appear in the attribute of pride and self-admiration. As a result, cries arise from within them: "I", "No one but me", "Who is like me?", "There is nobody like me." The masters have stressed humility to the degree of deprecation in order to get rid of this illness and eliminate this plague in the hope that the disciples might approach the measure of equilibrium.

The person who has humility may observe this equilibrium and conceive of it with respect to himself. However, with respect to the people, he must accommodate himself to their conception of him and of themselves, so that they will be at ease with him and he with them. This is what is meant by Sohrawardi's

---

1. Allusion to the satans who manage to slip by the guardians of the celestial spheres and listen to the goings on among the angels (Koran XV:18).

words, "He who wins the treasure of humility and wisdom will present himself to each person as that person evaluates him and will evaluate each person as that person evaluates himself. He who is provided with this has gained ease and relief, but no one understands it except the gnostics."

MH 351-53

Ansāri writes:

The Koran says, "The servants of the All-Merciful are those who walk in the earth modestly" (XXV:63). Humility is for the servant to abase himself before God's force. It has three degrees.

The first degree is humility before religion. It is that one does not bring rational arguments to bear against what has been transmitted, have doubts about a proof of religion, or see any way toward opposition. But none of this is correct for the servant unless he khows that salvation lies in insight, constancy comes after confidence, and clear signs stand above arguments.

The second degree is that you are content to have as your brothers those whom God is content to have as His servants, that is to say, the Moslems; that you reject no right of your enemy, and that you accept the excuses of him who offers them.

The third degree is that you abase yourself before God, thereby giving up your own view in service, the vision of your own right in companionship, and your own designation in witnessing.

MS 46-47

The Thirty-second Field is humility. From the Field of Poverty is born the Field of Humility. The Koran says, "The servants of the All-Merciful are those who walk in the earth modestly" (XXV:63). Humility is to stand in lowliness before the Truth. It is three things: Toward God, toward His religion, and toward His friends.

Humility toward His religion is three things: You do not hold your own opinion in face of His words, you do not seek a teacher above His Prophet, and you do not reject the right of your enemy.

Humility toward His friends is three things: You consider their worth greater than your own, you honor them more than yourself, and you keep free from thinking bad things about them.

Humility before God is three things: You are abject before His command, wilted before His decree, and present in His remembrance.

SM 361

—VI—

HUMBLENESS

khoshu'

Humbleness (*khoshu'*) means abject humility. In the terminology of the sufis it means that the heart stands before God's threshold ready for obedience and bent low in humility.

SIGNS OF HUMBLENESS

"It has been said that one of the signs of humbleness is that when people make the servant angry or oppose or reject him, he receives it as acceptance."

RQ I 427; TJ

THE DIFFERENCE BETWEEN HUMBLENESS AND HUMILITY

Humbleness is to follow God, while humility is to submit oneself to Him and to refrain from protesting against His decree.

RQ I 427

In the technical terminology of the people of the Truth, humbleness is to follow God.

TJ

In the early stages humbleness is the subjection of the limbs to acts of obedience; in the final stages it is to be disengaged from the residue of formal designations and from taking into account duality.

RSh IV 172

Asked about humbleness, Ḥasan Baṣri replied, "It is a fear that stands in the heart, while the heart clings to it."

TA 46

Dho'n-Nun said, "Every day the gnostic is more humble, since every hour he is nearer [to God]."

TSS 32

Abu Solaimān Dārāni said, "Everything has an adornment, and the adornment of truthfulness is humbleness."

TSS 73

Asked about humbleness, a sufi replied, "It is for the heart to stand before God with gathered aspiration."

RQ I 427

Sahl ebn 'Abdo'llāh said, "When a person's heart is humble, Satan does not come near him."

RQ I [1940] 74

Mohammad ebn 'Ali Termedhi said, "In the humble person the fires of passion have been extinguished, the smoke of the breast has been stopped, and the light of reverence has dawned in the heart, so passion has died and the heart has come to life; hence his limbs are humble."

RQ I 427

Asked about humbleness, Jonaid replied, "The lowliness of hearts before the Knower of Unseen Things."

RQ I 428

They have all agreed that the place of humbleness is the heart. One of them saw a man outwardly contracted, visibly broken, his shoulders pulled together. He said to him, "My friend, humbleness is here," pointing to his breast, "not here," pointing to his shoulders.

RQ I 428

It has been said that humbleness is to bow down in one's inmost consciousness on condition of courtesy before the witnessing of God.

RQ I 429

It has been said that humbleness is the melting and disappearing of the heart before the Truth's overpowering authority.

RQ I 429

It has been said that humbleness is the early stages of the overwhelming effects of awe (*haibat*).

RQ I 429

It has been said that humbleness is a trembling that enters the heart all at once when the truth is suddenly unveiled.

RQ I 429

SAYINGS OF MASTERS ABOUT HUMBLENESS

Shaykh Ruzbehān writes:

When a person's heart becomes limpid through the light of sadness and his inmost consciousness is purified through the brilliance of nearness, the splendor of the Attributes of God in the robes of Grandeur falls upon his spirit and he sees with the eye of penitence the force of eternity's majesty. Humbled are his inmost consciousness in eternity without beginning, his spirit in eternity without end, his heart in the spiritual realm (*malakut*), and his intellect in the realm of compulsion (*jabarut*). Then these lights pervade the existence of his outward form, which fluctuates, serene in servanthood (*'obudiyat*), broken before Lordship (*robubiyat*), humble in obedience, still beneath the streams of power; in his station of bewilderment he cannot bear to attend to the six directions because of the sparkling of the lights of Grandeur from every atom of his existence. The Prophet said of the person at prayer, "Were his heart to be humble, his limbs would be humble."

MA 30-31

Anṣāri writes:

The Koran says, "Is it not time that the hearts of those who have faith should be humbled to the remembrance of God and the truth which He has sent down?" (LVII:16). Humbleness is the extinction of the *nafs* and

100

the subsiding of the natural faculties in the face of something great or terrifying. It has three degrees:

The first degree is lowliness before the [Divine] Command, submission to the decree, and abasing oneself before the gaze of God.

The second degree is to watch out for the plagues of the *nafs* and actions, to see the bounty of everyone who has shown bounty to you, and to inhale the breeze of annihilation.

The third degree is to maintain reverence during unveiling, to purify the present moment of dissemblance before people, and to disengage one's vision of bounty [from all things except God].

MS 21-22

The Thirty-seventh Field is humbleness. From the Field of Sympathy (*eshfāq*) is born the Field of Humbleness. Humbleness is a fear that softens thought with reverence, refines moral traits, and teaches courtesy to the limbs. The Koran says, "Is it not time that the hearts of those who have faith should be humbled to the remembrance of God?" (LVII:16). Humbleness is dread along with awareness and resignation. It has three gates: Preferring others and tolerance in interactions, resignation and presence in service, and shame and veneration in the inmost consciousness.

The marks of preferring others in interactions are three: Bad people are secure from him, good people are happy with him, and God's creatures are free of him.

The sign of presence in service is three things: A sweetness which allows him no rest away from the Threshold, attention toward the goal so that he does not turn away from it to busy himself with the created realm, and a clear view of [his own] shortcomings so that he does not see himself as being in the right.

The sign of veneration is three things: Seeing God near oneself, seeing oneself far from God, and honoring His trials.

SM 291

اخلاص

—VII—

SINCERITY

ekhlāṣ

Ask the heart to give witness
to our sincerity, then look:
Everything there shows itself
in the mirror of my face.

Ḥāfeẓ

Sincerity (*ekhlās*) is that, without paying attention to
any creature or taking into account the gratification of
your own self, you think, do, and act for God.

THE DIFFERENCE BETWEEN SINCERITY
AND TRUTHFULNESS

"The difference between sincerity and truthfulness
(*ṣedq*) is that sincerity is the root and the principle,
while truthfulness is the branch and the corollary.
Another difference is that sincerity becomes manifest
after a person begins to act."

KF

105

THE DIFFERENCE BETWEEN
SINCERITY AND HYPOCRISY

Ja'far Kholdi said, "The difference between hypocrisy and sincerity is that the hypocrite performs actions to be seen while the sincere person performs actions to attain to God."

TSS 456

THE SIGN OF SINCERITY

Dho'n-Nun Meṣri said, "Three signs of sincerity are: Seeing the praise and the blame of the common people as the same, forgetting to see actions while doing the actions, and forgetting that actions demand reward in the next world."

RQ II 445

THE KINDS OF SINCERITY

'Ezzo'd-Din Kāshāni writes:
Whatever appears from the servant, word or act, action or state, has one face turned toward creation and another toward God. A person who devotes himself sincerely (akhlas) to the face of God to the exclusion of the face of creation is called sincere (mokhleṣ), while his act is known as sincerity (ekhlāṣ).

Sincerity is divided into two sorts: 'Sincerity' and 'sincerity in sincerity'.

As for 'sincerity', it is divided into four kinds, in respect of what appears from the servant. The first kind is sincerity in words. The servant devotes himself sincerely to considering the Act of God in the words which appear on his tongue to the exclusion of considering the act of his own self, and to considering God's gaze upon him to the exclusion of considering anyone else's gaze upon him....

The second kind is sincerity in acts, as in acts that are indifferent (mobāh).[1] The servant devotes himself sincerely to seeking the face of God's contentment in what he does, rather than seeking the face of his own gratification in this world by attracting benefits or repelling losses. Hence he only does what he does "for God's face" (LXXVI:9)....

The third kind is sincerity in actions, as in acts of worship prescribed in the Law. He devotes himself sincerely in each work to seeking the face of God's contentment, rather than the face of his own gratification, while waiting for the good reward in the next world....

The fourth kind is sincerity in states, like inspirations in the heart and influxes from the Unseen. He devotes himself sincerely in each state to the face of God's gaze toward him, rather than to the face of the gazes of God's creatures. He has no concern whatsoever for their gazes, since he is not concerned with their existence....

As for 'sincerity in sincerity', that is for the servant to devote himself sincerely to the face of God's Act in his sincerity, rather than to the face of his own act. He does not see the sincerity of his act, only the Act of God. So in truth the 'sincere one' (mokhles) is God, while the

1. Acts, it will be remembered, are divided into five categories according to Islamic law: the incumbent (wājeb), the recommended (mustahabb or mandub), the indifferent (mubāh), the reprehensible (makruh), and the unlawful (harām). The author is saying that these remarks pertain only to the middle category.

servant is 'made sincere' (*mokhlaṣ*). This is the ultimate degree of sincerity.

KW 358-59; KF 431

THE SINCERITY OF THE RIGHTEOUS

The possessor of sincerity in a work desires no compensation for it in this world or the next; this is the sincerity of the righteous (*ṣeddiqān*) . If a person performs actions in hope of paradise or fear of hell, he also is sincere, but he is not one of the righteous sincere. If a person performs a work sheerly for the sake of hypocrisy, he is situated among the perishing. The meaning of sincerity is expressed in the saying, "The sincere is that through which the face of God is desired." It is also expressed in Rowaim's saying: "Sincerity is that its possessor not be content with any compensation in the two worlds or any gratification in the two Kingdoms."

KF 432

SINCERITY OF THE COMMON AND THE ELECT

Abu 'Othmān Maghrebi said, "In sincerity the *nafs* has no gratification in any state; this is the sincerity of the common people. As for the sincerity of the elect, it is that everything which takes place in them does not take place through them. Acts of obedience appear from them, but they are detached from the acts. They do not see them nor take them into account."

RQ II 445

DEFINITIONS OF SINCERITY BY
THE MASTERS OF THE PATH

Literally sincerity means to refrain from hypocrisy in acts of obedience. Technically it means to purify the heart of the blemish of contaminants which spoil its clarity. More precisely: Everything can be conceived of as being contaminated by other than itself; when it is clarified and purified of that contamination, it is called pure (*khāles*). Thus an act that is purified (*mokhallas*) is called an act of sincerity (*ekhlās*). The Koran says, "What is in the bellies of cattle between filth and blood — pure milk" (XVI:66), for the purity of milk is that it should not be contaminated by filth and blood.

TJ

Fodhail ebn 'Eyādh said, "Refraining from actions for the sake of the people is hypocrisy, while performing them for their sake is to associate others with God; sincerity is that God releases you from both."

RQ II 446

It has been said, "Sincerity is that you seek no witness for your actions but God."

TJ

Fodhail ebn 'Eyādh said, "Sincerity is when man's outward and his inward, his stillness and his movement, are purely for God, not stained by gratification of the *nafs*, passion, creation, or desire."

TSS 471

Abu 'Abdo'llāh Basri said, "The shadows of your

hypocrisy disappear from the heart only through the light of sincerity, and the shadows of falsehood only through the light of truthfulness."

TSS 432

Ahmad Antāki said, "The most useful sincerity is that which negates from you hypocrisy, self-display, and pretension."

TSS 128

Dho'n-Nun said, "He who is intimate with God's creatures has taken over the carpet of the Pharoahs, while he who has ceased to see himself has taken over sincerity. When a person's share of things is He, he has no concern for anything less that may have slipped by."

TSS 29

Hāreth Mohāsebi said, "When a person rectifies his inward being through meditation and sincerity, God will adorn his outward with struggle and following the Prophet's Custom (sonnat)."

TSA 89

Sincerity is that you see no one else when you interact with Him and that you have chivalry toward others so that you are never unpleasant.

TSA 320

Rowaim said, "Sincerity is the disappearance of your own vision of the act." In other words when you see your own act, you see yourself, and the self-seer does not see God.

Ebn 'Atā' was asked, "Which action is sincere?" He replied, "That which is purified from plagues." The plagues that ruin actions are the self-admiration of the *nafs*, hypocrisy toward others, desiring compensation, and seeing the action, since each of these plagues destroys the obedience of the two worlds. Once the servant has escaped from these plagues, he is sincere.

KST 300

Jonaid said, "Sincerity is that through which God is desired, whatever the action may be."

T 99

Abu Sa'id Kharrāz said, "The hypocrisy of the gnostics is better than the sincerity of the disciples."

RQ II 445

Abu 'Othmān Maghrebi said, "Sincerity is to forget the vision of God's creatures by continual gazing upon the bounty of the Creator."

RQ II 446

Hodhaifa Mar'ashi said, "Sincerity is that the servant's acts be the same outwardly and inwardly."

RQ II 446

Jonaid said, "Sincerity is a mystery between God and the servant; no angel knows it to write it down, no satan

111

to corrupt it, and no passion to deflect it."

Sahl ebn 'Abdo'lläh was asked, "What thing is hardest for the *nafs?*" He answered, "Sincerity, since the *nafs* has no share in it."

RQ II 446

Makhul said, "No servant ever had sincerity for forty days without the wellsprings of wisdom flowing forth from his heart onto his tongue."

RQ II 447

Yusof ebn Hosain said, "The rarest thing in this world is sincerity. No matter how much I struggle to throw hypocrisy out of my heart, it seems to grow up within it in another color."

RQ II 447; TA 388

Sincerity is that the servant in his obedience desires nearness to God and nothing else — not making a show before any created thing, the earning of respect from people, the love for praise from others, or anything other than nearness to God.

RQ II 443

I heard Abu 'Ali Daqqäq say, "Sincerity is to beware of taking any created thing into consideration, while truthfulness is to cleanse oneself of acquaintance with the *nafs.* Hence the sincere person has no hypocrisy, while the truthful person has no self-admiration."

RQ II 444

Abu Bakr Daqqāq said, "Every sincere person is imperfect in his sincerity through the vision of his sincerity. If God wants to make his sincerity sincere, He eliminates his vision of his sincerity from his sincerity; then he is 'made sincere' (*mokhlas*), not 'being sincere' (*mokhles*)."

RQ II 445

Sahl ebn 'Abdo'llāh said, "No one recognizes hypocrisy but he who is sincere."

RQ II 445

Rowaim said, "Sincerity in actions is that the servant has no eye for compensation in either world."

TA 486

Abu Moḥammad Jorairi said, "Sincerity is the fruit of certainty, hypocrisy of doubt."

TA 581

Abo'l-Ḥasan Kharaqāni said, "I did not see my own actions as sincere, for then I would have seen someone other than He. Since I saw all as He, sincerity appeared."

TA 682

Abo'l-Ḥasan Kharaqāni said, "When you do something while seeing God, that is sincerity, but when you do something while seeking the creatures, that is hypocrisy. What need is there in the midst for creatures? God is the place for sincerity."

TA 710

Ebrāhim Adham said, "Sincerity is truthfulness of intention with God."

TA 112

Hātem Aṣamm said, "The beginning of renunciation is reliance upon God, its intermediate stage patience, and its end sincerity."

TA 302

Sahl ebn 'Abdo'llāh said, "Sincerity is response. Whoever does not respond is not sincere."

TA 320

Aḥmad Antaki said, "Sincerity is that when you perform an action, you do not think it right that people should remember you and think you great because of it; you do not seek the reward for your action from anyone except God. This is sincerity in actions."

TA 412

Jonaid said, "Sincerity is that you are annihilated from your own act; your act and your seeing it disappear."

TA 448

Jonaid said, "Sincerity is to remove creation from the interaction between God and self," since the self lays claim to Lordship.

TA 448

In the early stages sincerity is: "Let him [who hopes for the encounter with his Lord] perform righteous actions and not associate anyone with his Lord's worship" (XVIII:110). In the final stages sincerity is the profession of Divine Unity through the negation of dispersion (*farq*) from gathering (*jam'*) in the station of the unity of dispersion and gathering. Thus 'Ali has said, "[Sincerity is] a light that rises at the dawn of eternity-without-beginning, shining its traces upon the temples of the profession of Divine Unity."

RSh IV 174

Ruzbehān writes, "When the gnostic remains in the gratifications of love and the pleasures of witnessing, he becomes veiled by them from perceiving the mysteries of the profession of Eternity's Unity; then it becomes incumbent upon him to set him who professes Unity apart from his profession of it so that he will be pure (*khāles*) of his own self in his gnosis and sincere in freely giving away his existence through the attribute of being sanctified from attending to transitory things in his profession of Divine Unity. The Koran says, "Does not sincere religion belong to God?" (XXXIX:3). The Prophet said, "Sincerity is one of God's mysteries." The teacher says, "Sincerity is to set apart service and eliminate suspicion."

MA 38

Abu Sa'id Abo'l-Khair said, "When a person lives in the *nafs* he dies through death, but when he lives in sincerity and truthfulness he never dies; he is merely transferred from one house to another."

AT 305

Sincerity is to put all created things far from your

interaction with God.

THE DIFFERENCE BETWEEN SINCERITY AND TRUTHFULNESS ACCORDING TO JONAID

You asked about the difference between sincerity and truthfulness. The meaning of 'truthfulness' is to stand watch over the *nafs* by guarding and observing it; but first you must have fulfilled what is incumbent upon you according to the doctrine (*elm*) by setting up the proper bounds of outward states and having the right intention toward God at the outset of the act. Hence truthfulness is found within the reality of the attributes of will (*erādat*) when the will undertakes to perform those things to which God has directed you and to which you are called by your will's reality. To accomplish this you refuse to conform to the *nafs* when it seeks ease, since the doctrine has been drawn up for you and you conform to it and you refuse to interpret the texts on your own.

Hence 'truthfulness' exists before the reality of 'sincerity'. The Koran says, "That He might question the truthful concerning their truthfulness" (XXXIII:8). So He asked them what they wanted by their truthfulness after they had come to possess truthfulness. In another place the Koran refers to the truthful in a different sense: "This is the day the truthful shall be profited by their 'truthfulness'. [For them await gardens underneath which rivers flow, therein dwelling forever and ever]" (V:122).

In its first sense truthfulness is a mark that separates the created beings from sincerity, since sincerity exists as an attribute of the creature in two states: In the state of belief and intention, and in the state of acts and practices. Sincerity as an attribute of the truthful person exists in his belief without being ascribed to truthfulness except inasmuch as the beginnings of sincerity exist within him. He still must gain knowledge of how things happen when he carries out acts with his limbs and he must purify his acts of the impediments that are opposed to sincerity before he can be called 'sincere'.

The first step in sincerity is to devote oneself exclusively to God through the will, and the second step is to rid one's acts of plagues.

That which is 'truthfulness' in the eyes of God's creatures is different from 'sincerity', but that which is 'truthfulness' in the eyes of God is accompanied by 'sincerity'. It may be said that someone is 'truthful' when it is seen that he possesses the attributes of knowing the doctrine and striving to the utmost [in actions], but it is not said that he is 'sincere', since God's creatures can have no knowledge of his sincerity. Hence truthfulness is observed in the attributes of the truthful person, but sincerity does not exist in that which can be observed. So the truthful person is described by the beauty of the attributes of his visible mien and ascribed to truthfulness by the indications of his outward aspect, while the beginnings of sincerity exist within him. But he still must gain knowledge of how things happen when they come to him. He accepts what conforms with his original intention and rejects that which opposes his outward doctrine.

Sincerity is higher than truthfulness because there is added knowledge, the power to reject the whispering of the enemy whom the servant faces, and clarity of the

117

heart. But nothing is higher than sincerity, since the servant can have no goal in servanthood beyond sincerity. One does not speak of 'the sincerity of the sincere', since there is no goal beyond sincerity. The Koran says, "That He might question the truthful concerning their truthfulness" (XXXIII:8); it does not say, "That He might question the sincere concerning their sincerity," since sincerity is God's goal for the creatures in that which He has called them to worship. Hence it is higher than truthfulness, and truthfulness lies below it.

'Truthfulness' is applied to three cases: The person who is truthful with his tongue and who speaks the truth, whether or not it be to his advantage, by leaving aside interpretation and falsification; the person who is truthful in his acts and who strives to the utmost to dislodge himself from ease; and the person who is truthful in his heart and who has the intention to go toward God through his acts. When a person possesses these traits he is 'truthful', though truthfulness exists in the truthful person in every state; he is not free from it in any one of his states....

So truthfulness is found in exercising abstinence, ascetic practice, renunciation, trust, contentment, love, yearning, and the profession of Divine Unity for all those who perform the ritual prayer, in the attributes of the disciple and the master, and in the rememberer and the Remembered; in every case an outward and visible mien will be found giving witness that the person is truthful.

The meaning of 'sincerity' is to devote the intention exclusively to God and to aim for Him correctly, while the intellect is present when things come to the intellect must clarify the fluctuation of affairs through that which is in conformity with the servant's sound intention, rejecting what is opposed to the intention, that is, that which comes from the *nafs* and the enemy. At the same time the servant must see God's kindness and stop seeing the *nafs*; by correct knowledge of God's 'bounty he must maintain good composure when others blame him, while detesting their praise for him out of fear that his gnosis may be corrupted; and he must cease seeing created things when he meets different sorts of states. This knowledge can be observed in the sincere witness, but it is absent from him who witnesses the

Hence truthfulness and sincerity come together in the state of the sincere person, while truthfulness stands alone in the truthful person, though he has the beginnings of sincerity. The utmost quality of those who are described by servanthood in their seeking to worship is sincerity. In the reality of his truthfulness the truthful person is charged with sincerity, while in the reality of his sincerity the sincere person is charged with sufficiency because of his penetrating insight — for in the reality of his insight's penetration the person of insight is charged with guarding everything that is in danger of corruption. Then through being in charge he gains mastery; he overcomes the intellect and annihilates its opposition to what he has found. As a result of taking charge in this specific sense, he ceases worshiping God through his *nafs* and enters into worship of Him through Oneness. When this occurs, it is the reality of the profession of Divine Unity of the elect, achieved through the disappearance of the vision of things because of the arising of the vision of God. The person's states flow over him in accordance with the while the attributes of these states have fallen away.

When the servant reaches this stage, he leaves aside the attributes of those things that can be described by intellect, so intellect's proposals in face of the existence of the reality of the profession of Divine Unity become devilish whisperings that must be rejected, since intellect supported the servant in respect of his being a servant when he undertook servanthood, but when the realities of his disposition fell upon him from God, he entered into servanthood from a source different from the first. Hence he exists in attribute but does not drink from the same source. At this point he is found/lost.

RJ 47-51

ANṢARI'S EXPLANATION OF SINCERITY

The Koran says, "Does not sincere religion belong to God?" (XXXIX:3). Sincerity is to purify actions from every contamination. It has three degrees.

The first degree is to dislodge the seeing of actions from the actions, to be rid of seeking compensation for actions, and to renounce contentment with actions.

The second degree is to be ashamed of one's actions while striving to the utmost, to increase effort while protecting oneself against vision [of effort], and to see actions as God's sheer munificence in the light of God-given success.

The third degree is to devote oneself sincerely to actions by being rid of actions: You let them go forward in the route of the doctrine, while you yourself go forward witnessing God's decree and freed of the

120

Will of his Master, bondage of designation.

The Twenty-fifth Field is Sincerity. From the Field of Conformity is born the Field of Sincerity. The Koran says, "Say: 'God I worship, devoting my religion sincerely to Him'" (XXXIX:14). Sincerity means 'to make pure'. It has three kinds: Sincerity of testimony, which is in submission (*eslām*); sincerity of service, which is in faith (*imān*), and sincerity of gnosis, which is in true reality (*haqiqat*).

Sincerity of testimony has three witnesses: Striving in His command, respect for His prohibition, and taking ease in His contentment: "Does not sincere religion belong to God?" (XXXIX:3).

Sincerity of service has three witnesses: Not seeing creation while worshiping God, observing the Prophet's Custom (*sonnat*) in God's work, and finding sweetness in God's service. In the words of the Koran, "They were commanded only to worship God, devoting the religion sincerely to Him" (XCVIII:5).

Sincerity of knowledge has three witnesses: A fear that holds one back from sins, a hope that keeps one in obedience, and a love that finds God's decree delicious. In the words of the Koran, "Assuredly We purified them with a quality of sincerity" (XXXVIII:46).

SM 322-23

استـقامت

—VIII—

CONSTANCY

estegāmat

He said, "Where's the plague?"
I said, "In the lane of Thy love."
He said, "How are you there?"
I said, "Constant."

Rumi

In the language of the doctors of the Shari'at,
constancy (*esteqāmat*) is to remain firm and steady in
following God's commands and prohibitions so as not
to neglect any of them or to deviate from the Straight
Path (*as-serāt al-mostaqim*).[1] In sufi terminology it is to
remain firm and steady in love for God, so that the
person has no fear in whatever affliction might arrive; on
the contrary, he takes it as the cure for his pain.

1. The Straight Path (*as-serāt al-mostaqim*) is mentioned in about
thirty verses of the Koran; the term normally calls to mind the first
sura, which is recited by every Muslim in his daily prayers and
which includes the verse, "Lead us on the Straight Path" (I:5).
'Straight' (*mostaqim*) is the adjective derived from 'constancy'.
Hence one could translate the verse as, "Lead us on the path of
constancy"; alternatively, one could translate 'constancy'
throughout this section as 'straightness'.

125

In the *Ṣaḥiḥ* of Moslem the following hadith is recorded: "A person said to the Messenger of God, 'Tell me a word about Islam concerning which I will never have to ask anyone after you.' The Prophet replied: 'Say, "I have faith in God", then remain constant.'"[1]

THE KINDS OF CONSTANCY

Yaḥyā ebn Mo'ādh said, "Constancy is of three kinds: Constancy of the tongue in professing the faith (*shahādat*), constancy of the inward being in the truthfulness of the will (*erādat*), and constancy of the limbs in performing worship."

KF

In constancy the children of Adam are of seven kinds: Constant in word, constant in act, constant in heart (*qalb*); constant in word and act without heart, in act and heart without word, or in word and heart without act; or constant in word, in act, and in state in keeping with the words of the Koran, "Be constant as thou wert commanded" (XI:112). What is meant is that the servant meditates on God in his fluctuation.

> He is constant who has experienced
> his resurrection without death,
> and no one knows him.
> Nothing created, neither wife nor child,
> turns him away

1. SMS, *Imān* 62.

126

from the affair of his Creator.

RSh I 250

THE DEGREES OF CONSTANCY

I heard the master Abu 'Ali Daqqāq say, "Constancy has three degrees: Setting up *(taqwim)*, establishing *(eqāmat)*, and constancy itself. Setting up has to do with teaching courtesy to the soul, establishing with refinement of the heart, and constancy with bringing the inmost consciousness near [to God]."

RQ 441

CONSTANCY OF THE BEGINNERS
AND THE ADVANCED

Constancy is a degree which perfects and completes all things. Its existence actualizes and puts in correct order all good. If a person's state is not constant, he has wasted his exertion and effort. The Koran says, "Be not as a woman who tears her thread into fibers after it was strong" (XVI:92). Whoever is not constant in his attributes will not ascend from the station he occupies to another, nor will his wayfaring be built upon a sound foundation.

In order to be a novice, one must have constancy in the rules of the early stages, just as the gnostic must have constancy in the various kinds of courtesy in the final stages. One of the signs of constancy in beginners is that no lassitude stains their dedication to actions;

those in the intermediate stages do not halt in their waystations; as for those at the end of the path, no veil interferes with their Union.

RQ II 440-41

CONSTANCY DEFINED BY THE MASTERS

Moḥammad ebn Faḍhl Balkhi said, "That thing whose existence makes all good things good and whose nonexistence makes all ugly things ugly is constancy."

TSA 306

Companionship with God is two words: Consent and constancy — consent to the covenant and constancy in fulfilling it.[1]

TSA 502

Abu 'Amr Nojaid said, "When a person has constancy ['straightness'],[2] no one will go crooked because of him, and when a person has gone crooked, no one will gain constancy through him."

TSS 480

Shebli said, "Constancy is that you see the present moment as a resurrection."

RQ II 442

It has been said that constancy in words is to refrain from backbiting, in acts to negate innovation, in action

---

1. Allusion to Koran II:40: "Fulfill My covenant, and I shall fulfill your covenant."
2. Cf. footnote 1, p. 125.

128

to negate lassitude, and in states to negate the veil.

RQ II 442

The master Abu Bakr Moḥammad ebn Faurak said,
"The *s* in *esteqāmat* [constancy] is known [gram-
matically] as the '*s* of seeking', so the sense is: They
should seek from God that He establish (*eqāmat)* them in
their profession of Divine Unity, then in the maintenance
of their covenants and the keeping of their bounds."

RQ II 442

Abu ʿAli Jauzjāni said, "Be the owner of constancy,
not the seeker of charismatic gifts (*karāmat*), for your
nafs is set in motion by the seeking of charismatic gifts,
but your Lord demands constancy from you."

RQ II 441

It has been said that no one is capable of constancy
but the great ones, since it is to leave aside familiar
things, to separate oneself from designations and habits,
and to undertake before God the reality of truthfulness.

RQ II 441

Abu ʿAli Daqqāq said, "If a person does not have
constancy with God in the beginning, he will not sit with
Him at the end. If he is constant in the way of spiritual
struggle, at the end he will sit in witnessing."

TA 653

Asked about constancy, Shebli said, "It is to see the

129

to undertake everything which God commands."

TA 633

Abu Bakr Wāseṭi said, "That characteristic through which good things are perfected and through the lack of which all good things become ugly is constancy, for it takes you away from the share of the *nafs* and opens you up to what will be your own share."

TA 747

Abu Saʻid said, "Constancy is that, having said 'One,' you no longer say 'Two.' But the creatures and God are two."

AT 296

Constancy is to fulfill all covenants and to hold fast to the Straight Path while observing the mean in all things, such as food, drink, clothing, and every affair of religion and this world. This is the Straight Path, like the Straight Path in the next world.[1] Hence the Prophet said, "The sura *Hud* has turned my hair white,"[2] since within it were sent down the words, "Be constant as thou wert commanded" (XI:112).

TJ

---

1. Reference to the Straight Path which bridges hell. According to authoritative *hadiths*, it is thin as a thread and sharp as a sword for the unbelievers, but wide and easy for the faithful.
2. *Hud* is the eleventh sura of the Koran. The *hadith*, as found in one of the authoritative collections (ST, *Tafsir* LVI, 6), also mentions four other suras (LVI, LXXVII, LXXVII, LXXXI).

resurrection in this world." He also said, "Constancy is

Constancy is to combine the performance of acts of obedience with the avoidance of acts of disobedience. It has been said that constancy is the opposite of deviation. It is for the servant to walk on the path of obedience according to the guidance of the Law and intellect. It has also been said that constancy is that you never choose anything over God.

TJ

In the early stages constancy is to fulfill the covenant of repentance and to remain firm in it. In the final stages it is to be constant both in subsistense, after annihilation in God and in traveling to God. It is to travel to God through a witnessing of Him that exists through Him.

RSh IV 174

STATEMENTS OF THE MASTERS OF
THE PATH ABOUT CONSTANCY

Ruzbehān writes:

When gnosis and love have become the gnostic's natural disposition, when he suffers no outward lassitude or inward heedlessness of God, when in sobriety distractions and trials do not change him, and when in intoxication the *nafs*, Satan, and passion do not veil him from witnessing, then he stands within the bounds of constancy. God said to His Prophet, "Be constant as thou wert commanded" (XI:112). Since the Prophet knew what God meant by the command and he recognized that the reality of constancy is to emerge from God's trials and to witness Him in all situations, whether moving or still, he said, "*Hud* has turned my

131

hair white." Moḥammad ebn Faḍhl said, "The trait that perfects all good things is constancy." The gnostic says: "In constancy the heaviest influxes of theophany work in the mode of sobriety."

MA 148

Shāh Ne'mato'llāh Wali writes:
'Constancy'[1] is a wisdom that permeates all created things, as the Koran says: "Our Lord is He who gave each thing its creation, then guided" (XX:50). The 'constancy' of a plant is for its movement to be inverted, since it pulls water up from the roots to the branches and produces useful and delicious or bad tasting fruit. If an animal moved upward and stood on two legs like a human being, a rider could not be at ease on it, nor would it be able to carry heavy burdens on its back.

The Wise Creator brought each thing into existence with a known motion in accordance with a complete, extensive, and exhaustive wisdom so that through this motion the desired benefit may accrue. Motion in the middle is known as 'straight' ['constant'] motion, while motion away from the middle is ascending motion and motion toward the middle is descending motion. Descending motion is angelic and divine, while ascending motion is human.

1. Throughout this passage the author is paying attention to the literal sense of the term *esteqāmat* or 'constancy', that is, 'straightness' and 'uprightness'. Cf. footnote no. 1, p. 125. The passage is based on FM II 217.26.

Look at 'constancy' in all things —
　　Take a glance at our drunken eye!

The curve of a bow lies in its 'straightness'.

　　The bow is 'straight' because it's crooked —
　　The arrow went 'straight' to the target.

Human motion is 'straight' both in form and
meaning, while the motion of a plant — and also an
animal — is inverted in the sensory realm but 'straight'
rationally. So 'constancy' pervades all entities, whether
substance or accident, state or word, while the Lord of
the Worlds is on a Straight Path in respect of Lordship,
as is said in the Koran: "There is no creature that crawls
but He takes it by the forelock. Surely my Lord is on a
straight path" (XI:56).

　　We take 'straightness' from Him —
　　He's on a Straight Path, and we tag along.

RSh IV 268-69

Anṣārī writes:
The Koran says, "Be constant toward Him!" (XLI:6).
The words "toward Him" point to exclusive devotion.
　　Constancy is a spirit which gives life to states, just as
it nurtures the actions of the common people. It is a
middle domain between the hollows of dispersion and
the high ground of gathering. It has three degrees:
　　The first degree is constancy in striving in the middle
course, not transgressing the delineations of the
doctrine, nor going outside the bounds of sincerity, nor
opposing the way of the Prophet's Custom.

133

The second degree is constancy in states, which is to witness Reality, but not as an acquisition; to reject claims for oneself, but not just theoretically; and to remain with the light of wakefulness, but not with the effort of vigilance.

The third degree is constancy through refraining from seeing constancy, through being absent from seeking constancy, and through witnessing God's establishing *(eqāqmat)* and His setting up *(taqwim)* — mighty is His Name!

MS 32-33

The Twenty-eighth Field is constancy. From the Field of Resolve (*'azm)* is born the Field of Constancy. The Koran says, "Be constant as thou wert commanded" (XI:112). Constancy is to accompany without fluctuation. It is of three kinds: The constancy of acts, the constancy of moral traits, and the constancy of breaths.

The constancy of acts is possessed by the pious, or else they are hypocrites. The constancy of moral traits is possessed by those who have certitude, or else that have gone astray. The constancy of breaths is possessed by the gnostics, or else they are impostors.

Constancy of acts has three witnesses: The servant's outward being conforms [with the Law], his inward is sincere, and he accepts blame as his reward.

Constancy of moral traits has three signs: If people are cruel toward you, you ask their pardon; if they torment you, you give thanks; and if they become sick, you go to visit them.

Constancy of breaths has three witnesses: You watch over each breath, in order to gain worth; you consider your lifetime a single breath, in order to become free; and you scrutinize the breath, in order to become fulfilled.

Know that at each passing breath your life is either a disputant or an intercessor. With each breath God shows kindness to the servant, while in face of that the servant sins. A miserable breath is the smoke of a snuffed-out lamp in a narrow, doorless room, while a fortunate breath is a radiant fountain in a garden adorned with fruit.

SM 326-27

ادب

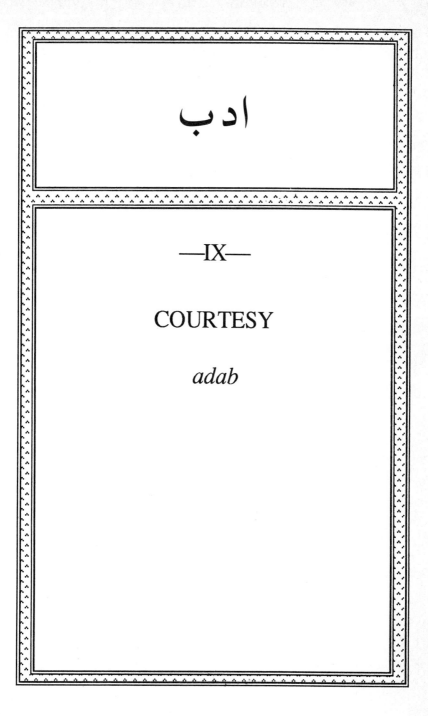

—IX—

COURTESY

adab

Step not into the Tavern of Ruin without courtesy —
Its inhabitants are the confidants of the King!

Ḥāfeẓ

In sufi terminology, courtesy (*adab*) is for the adept
to observe his duties in words, acts, and states, and to
maintain his own limits in every station, both with God
and His creatures, inwardly and outwardly. To observe
outward courtesy is required in the state of awareness
and sobriety, but when the reins of free choice have left
the sufi's hand and heart in the state of intoxication, he
cannot be expected to observe it. As Rumi says in the
famous story of Moses and the shepherd,

O Moses, those who know courtesy's rules
    are one thing,
those whose spirits and souls burn
    are something else.

M II 1765

In the words of Ḥāfeẓ:

I had a thousand intellects and courtesies, master,
but now that I'm drunk and ruined —
welcome, discourtesy!

Some have held that in the circles of the people of
heart, one must observe inward courtesy, but not the
outward kind. This is not correct. It is true that Rumi has
written the following:

Before the people of heart,
courtesy is shown inwardly,
for their hearts are aware
of secret thoughts.

M II 3220

But Rumi means that it is not sufficient to observe
only outward courtesy before the masters of the Path; on
the contrary, there must be inward courtesy as well.

TALES OF COURTESY

O traveler on the Path,
if you have news of God's secret,
show courtesy
to the beggars in the tavern!

Ḥāfeẓ

140

It is told that once Sari Saqati was discoursing on the meaning of patience. In the midst of his words a scorpion crawled up his leg and began to sting him, but he continued to speak without showing discomfort until it stung him several times. Those assembled asked him, "Why did you not drive it away from yourself?" He replied, "I was ashamed before God lest I speak about a state and then go against what I know about it."

MH 203

Once a darvish was asked, "What is poverty?" He replied, "Wait a moment until I go and return." Having gone and come back he said, "Poverty is that you own nothing." They asked him, "Why did you delay in answering?" He said, "I had one dirham in my possession. I did not want to speak about poverty while possessing something; I wanted my words to conform to my acts."

MH 204

Abu 'Obaid Qāsem ebn Salām said, "Once I was God's neighbor in Mecca; sometimes when relieving nature I would sit facing the Ka'ba and sometimes I would sleep on my back with my feet in the direction of the Ka'ba. Then one day 'A'esha of Mecca, who was one of the female gnostics, gave me some good counsel. She said, 'Abu 'Obaid, it is said that you are one of the men of knowledge. Accept from me some words: Do not sit with God except with courtesy. Otherwise your name will be erased from the book of nearness.'"

MH 206-207

Sari Saqaṭi said, "Once after finishing my litanies I stretched my feet in the direction of the prayer niche. Suddenly I heard a voice saying, 'Sari, is that how you sit with kings?' I immediately pulled my feet to myself and said, 'By Thy Might, after this I will never stretch out my legs!'" Jonaid said, "Sixty years later he was still alive and had never stretched out his legs, neither by day nor by night."

MH 205

It is told of Jonaid that he said, "Once I was in the Shuniziya Mosque with a group of people waiting for a funeral procession to arrive so that we could say the prayer for the dead. I saw a poor man enter the mosque and begin to beg from those within it. It crossed my mind that it would be better for this man to take a job and remove the burden that he places on others. That night I dreamed that a corpse was placed before me and it was said, 'Eat of this!' I said, 'How can I eat the flesh of a corpse?' The reply came, 'Just as you ate it yesterday.'[1] When I looked, I saw that the corpse had the face of the man who had been begging in the mosque. I realized that this was the result of that thought about him that had crossed my mind. I said, 'I did not express that backbiting with my tongue, it only crossed my mind.' The answer came, 'Do you not know that the thought that crosses your mind is like an act in the case of

1. Reference to Islam's prohibition of backbiting (*ghiba*, Persian *ghaibat*), which is defined as saying something bad, albeit true, about a person behind his back; if the statement is false, it is called slander (*bohtān*) The Koran says, "Do not spy, neither backbite one another; would any of you like to eat the flesh of his brother dead?" (XLIX:12).

others?' I said, 'I repent of it.' Immediately the corpse was taken away."

MH 205-206

Abu Hafṣ Ḥaddād going on the *hajj* (pilgrimage) and came to Baghdad. Jonaid came to meet him. Abu Hafṣ was old and his students were standing around him showing great courtesy. Jonaid said, "Have you taught your companions the courtesy of kings?" Abu Hafṣ replied, "Observing outward courtesy toward God's friends is part of inward courtesy toward God."

TSA 114

THE DISCOURTESY OF DARVISHES

Abu Bakr Doqqi was asked about the discourtesy of darvishes toward God in their states. He replied, "They fall from the reality of knowledge to the outward form of knowledge."

TSA 507

THE KINDS OF PEOPLE IN COURTESY

Abu Naṣr Sarrāj said, "In courtesy people are of three kinds: First are the people of this world, for whom courtesy is rhetoric, eloquence, and the memorization of doctrine, formalities, the names of kings, and the poetry of the Arabs.[1] Second are the people of religion, for

---

1. *Adab* signifies courtesy, etiquette, correct demeanor, appropriate behavior, and ideal refinement of thoughts, words, actions, and moral traits. On the linguistic level, the term is often employed to refer to the cultured and refined knowledge of language and literature.

whom courtesy is discipline of the limbs, observation of the ordinances of the Law, refraining from passions, and training the *nafs*. Third are the people of election, for whom courtesy is purity of the heart, guarding the inmost consciousness, fulfilling covenants, preserving the present moment (*waqt*), disregarding scattered thoughts, and conducting oneself correctly in the place of seeking, the time of presence, and the station of nearness."

TA 640

COURTESY DEFINED BY SUFI MASTERS

Since every word, act, and state in every time and station has a special courtesy, it is impossible to enumerate all courtesy's rules. Here we have tried to record certain words of the masters, each of which was uttered in specific circumstances, so that, through the whole, the way and method of sufi courtesy can be understood. We also cite the following line of Rumi to show that the acts of courtesy of the darvishes are not concocted but rather intuited:

> The spirit learns
> > a thousand kinds of courtesy
> > > from love,
> A courtesy
> > not to be found
> > > in schools.

Mamshād Dinawari said, "The courtesy of the disciple lies in holding fast to reverence for masters, serving brothers, leaving aside secondary causes, and

144

maintaining the Law's rules of courtesy for himself."

TSS 320

In the early stages courtesy is to ascend from joy to the open plain of witnessing and to become clear of multiplicity in attributes; in the final stages it is to have no need for courtesy through God's making one courteous and to be rid of seeing courtesy.

RSh IV 176

Sari Saqati said, "Four traits lift up the servant: Knowledge, courtesy, trustworthiness, and continence (*effat*)."

TSS 44

Courtesy is to interact with God and to rise above water and clay and the frivolity of the *nafs*. You do not say, "I and my deeds," but "He and His favor and His giving success."

TSA 358

Abu 'Abdo' llāh Nebāji said, "Courtesy is the ornament of the free."

TSA 251

'Abdo'llāh ebn Mobārak said, "When a person is remiss in courtesy, he is punished by being deprived of the norms of the Prophet's Custom; when he is remiss in the norms of the Prophet's Custom, he is punished by being deprived of ob igatory actions (*farā'edh*); when he is remiss in obligatory actions, he is punished by being deprived of knowledge."

MH 207

'Abdo'llāh ebn Mobārak said, "People have multiplied their acts of courtesy, but we maintain that courtesy is the knowledge of the *nafs*." He means that the reason a person refrains from courtesy is ignorance, while the source of ignorance is the *nafs*. Whoever trains the *nafs* through knowledge becomes courteous.

MH 207

The word *adab* ('courtesy') expresses the beautification of moral traits (*akhlāq*) and the refinement of words and acts. Acts are of two kinds: Acts of the heart, which are known as intentions (*niyāt*), and acts of the bodily frame, which are known as actions (*a'māl*). Moral traits and intentions pertain to the inward, words and acts to the outward. Hence that person observes perfect courtesy whose outward and inward are adorned with the beautiful qualities of moral traits, words, intentions, and actions. His moral traits accord with his words, and his intentions conform to his actions. As he appears, he is, and as he is, he appears.

MH 203

Jonaid said, "Servanthood is to hold fast to courtesy, while rebellion is discourtesy."

MH 207

Abu 'Ali Daqqāq said, "Through his obedience the servant will reach the Garden, and through his courtesy in obedience, he will reach God."

MH 207

146

'Abdo'llāh ebn Mobārak said, "Courtesy in service is more precious than service."

MH 207

Anas ebn Mālek said, "Courtesy in an action is the sign that the action has been accepted [by God]."

MH 207

Jonaid said, "When love is genuine, the conditions for courtesy drop away."

RQ II 563

Abu 'Othmān Ḥiri said, "When love is genuine, holding fast to courtesy becomes imperative for the lover."

RQ II 563

Dho'n-Nun said, "When the disciple ceases being courteous, he returns from whence he came."

RQ II 563

The reality of courtesy is for all good traits to come together.

RQ II 558

Abu 'Ali Daqqāq said, "Refraining from courtesy is a tree whose fruit is expulsion. Whoever shows discourtesy on the carpet of kings is sent back to the gate, and whoever shows discourtesy at the gate is sent out to the stables."

He also said, "When a person is discourteous in

companionship, his ignorance has handed him over to being killed."

TA 653

Abo'l-Qāsem Naṣrābādi said, "If someone does not have courtesy of the soul, he cannot reach courtesy of the heart. And if someone does not have courtesy of the heart, how can he reach courtesy of the spirit? And if he does not have courtesy of the spirit, how can he reach the locus of nearness to God? Indeed, how is it possible that God's carpet should be turned over to him? That is, unless he should have gained the different kinds of courtesy and be trustworthy both secretly and openly."

TA 792

Abu 'Othmān Ḥiri said, "Courtesy is the hope of the poor and the adornment of the rich."

TA 482

Ebn 'Aṭā' said, "The *nafs* is kneaded of discourtesy, while the servant is commanded to hold fast to courtesy. The *nafs* goes after that from which it was kneaded in the field of opposition, while the servant strives to hold it back from seeking the bad. If a person lets go of the reins of the *nafs*, he is its partner in corruption."

TA 492

Ebn 'Aṭā' said, "Courtesy is to stop with everything considered good." When asked to explain he replied, "You act toward God with courtesy both secretly and openly. When you do so, you are a man of

148

even if you speak incorrect Arabic."[1]

RQ II 559

Courtesy is knowledge of that which will put you on your guard against every kind of offense.

TJ

For the people of the Law, courtesy is abstinence; for the people of wisdom it is to watch over the self.... The wise man says: "Courtesy is for the creatures to sit together on the carpet of veracity and to conform with the realities." The master of realization says: "Courtesy is to reject free choice and to plead on the carpet of poverty." It is in this sense that the poet has said,

> Courtesy is not to accomplish acts of worship
>> nor to strive in seeking the Truth.
> Other than becoming dust,
>> everything else is discourtesy.

KF

WORDS OF THE MASTERS ON COURTESY

Ruzbehän writes:
When the gnostic reaches the station of exaltation, God teaches him courtesy through inspiration, address, and speech. Greater than that, He teaches him courtesy through awe, the assault of Grandeur, and the shock of

---

1. Ebn 'Atā' alludes here to *adab* in the sense of correct and refined knowledge of the Arabic language (see footnote 1, p. 143).

149

gazing upon Might itself. The mightiest courtesy is that

his eye never glances at anything but God. Do you not
see how God described His beloved Moḥammad with
the words, "His eye swerved not, nor swept astray"
(LIII:17).[1] The Prophet said, "My Lord taught me
courtesy, so my courtesy is beautiful."[2] Daqqāq said,
"He who shows discourtesy to kings will perish with
those who perish." The gnostic says: "Courtesy in
gnosis is for him to be with God in accordance with
what God desires wherever and howsoever he might
be."

MA 141

Shāh Neʿmatoʾllāh writes:
The Messenger of God said, "Verily God taught me
courtesy" — that is, gathered within me everything good
— "so my courtesy is beautiful" — that is, He made me
the locus of every beautiful quality.

> Thus spoke the grandfather
>   of Ḥasan and Ḥosain;
> thus is the character
>   of Ḥasan and Ḥosain.

Courtesy is of several kinds:
Courtesy according to the Shariʿat involves the
commands of God's Messenger when he said, "Do such
and such." These commands pertain either to substance,

1. The verse refers to the vision of the Prophet during his ascent
(meʿraj) to God.
2. The hadith is found in JS I 224.

accident, time, place, position, relation, state, or number and quantity.[1]

As for courtesy in paying the religious tax (*zakāt*) on substances, whether minerals, plants, or animals —

> Whatever the Messenger of God has said,
> > give of that,
> to whomever he has said to entrust it,
> > that is best.

Courtesy in accidents pertains to the acts of the person for whom the Law has made prescriptions, that is, [the five legal categories of] incumbent, prohibited, recommended, reprehensible, and indifferent.

Courtesy of time pertains to the times of the acts of worship. Each time has a specific property relating to the person for whom the prescription has been made; some of the time periods are long while others are short.

Courtesy of place involves things like the places of performing acts of worship. The Koran says, "The places of prostration belong to God; so call not, along with God, upon anyone" (LXXII:18).

> In His house remember Him constantly —
> > Be careful to observe courtesy, and that's all.

---

1. This discussion is an abridgement of Chapter 202 of FM, where there is a clear presentation of all ten of Aristotle's categories. Though Shāh Ne'mato'llāh lists eight here, he only deals with seven in the text, at the end turning to the courtesies of service, which are outside the courtesies of the Shari'at.

Courtesy of position has to do with not changing the names which have been given to things and which have been designated as lawful or unlawful. The Messenger of God said, "A time will come upon people when tribes will appear who name wine by another name in order to make it lawful through the name." In the same way wine has been called 'grape juice' and hypocrisy 'dissimulation', after which they were declared lawful through the name.

> To say such things
>   is to abandon courtesy.

An example of courtesy of relation is provided by the words of Abraham: "When I am sick, He heals me" (XXVI:80); or the words of Kheḍhr, "I desired to damage it" (XVIII:79), where he spoke in the first person, since rationally the act was blameworthy.

> Look at the courtesy of Kheḍhr,
>   look at the subtlety in this account!

Next Kheḍhr spoke in the plural, "We desired that their Lord should give to them one better in exchange" (XVIII:81), because praise and blame were shared. Finally he said, "Thy Lord desired that they should come of age" (XVIII:82), because building up the wall for the happiness of Moslem orphans calls for praise and commendation.

As for courtesy in numbers, this pertains to the acts

of the servants, such as ablutions, and the measures in them, as well as the number of prayers in the specified times according to the statutes of the Shari'at.

> Whatever they say, do it!
> Not more or less — do it like the gnostics.
> Be a follower of Muhammad's Shari'at;
> Whatever he commands, do it!

Then there is the courtesy of traveling in the service of kings. These are either the body's undertaking the duties of the statutes, that is, submission (*eslām*); the heart's undertaking to confirm the surrender, that is, faith (*imān*); or the spirit's undertaking to witness the All-Knowing King, that is, beneficence (*ehsān*).

"God's aid is there to be sought" (XII:18) and He is the trusted.

RSh IV 217-19

Ansāri writes:

The Koran says, "Those who keep God's bounds" (IX:112). Courtesy is to preserve the boundary between exaggerated attention and avoidance while knowing the harm of overstepping. It has three degrees:

The first degree is to prevent fear from passing into despair, to keep hope from leading to security, and to restrain joy lest it resemble boldness.

The second degree is to emerge from fear[1] into the field of contraction, to rise from hope to the field of expansion, and to ascend from joy to the field of witnessing.

1 On hope, fear, and expansion, see Nurbakhsh, *Sufism II*.

153

The third degree is the gnosis of courtesy, then to be without need for having courtesy because of God's teaching courtesy, then to be rid of seeing the burden of courtesy.

MS 52-53

The Fifty-fifth Field is Courtesy. From the Field of Beneficence is born the Field of Courtesy. The Koran says: "Those who keep God's bounds" (IX:112). Courtesy is to live within boundaries and to walk in measure. It takes place in three things: Service, gnosis, and interactions.

In service it is to struggle without affectation, to be cautious without lingering doubts, and to be generous without remiss.

In gnosis courtesy is three things: To have fear without despair, to have hope without security, and to be familiar without impudence.

In interactions courtesy is three things: Kind companionship without flattery, firmness without quarreling, and remembrance of favor without boasting.

SM 376-77

LIST OF SOURCES

Ansari, 'Abdo'llah, *Majmu'a-ye rasā'el-e Khwāja 'Abdo'llāh Ansāri*. Ed. M. Shirwāni. Tehran, 1352/1973.

_____. *Manāzel as-sā'erin*. Ed. S. Laugier de Beaurecueil. Cairo, 1962.

_____. *Sad maidān*. Ed. with *Manāzel as-sā'erin* by R. Farhādi. Kabul, 1355/1976.

_____. *Tabaqāt as-sufiya*. Ed. 'A. Habibi. Kabul, 1347 / 1968.

_____. *Tafsir-e 'erfāni wa adabi-ye Qor'ān majid* (recorded and revised by Ansāri's student Maibodi). Ed. H. Āmuzegār. Tehran, 1348/1969.

'Attār, Farido'd-Din. *Tadhkerat al-auliā* Ed. M. Este'lāmi. Tehran, 1346/1967.

Bākharzi, Abo'l-Mafākher. *Aurād al-ahbāb wa fosus al-ādāb*. Ed. I. Afshār. Vol. 2, Tehran, 1345/1966.

Bertels, Y.E. *Tasawwof wa adabiyāt-e tasawwof*. Persian translation from the Russian by S. Izadi. Tehran, 1356/1977. Includes the anonymous glóssary of sufi terminology, *Mer 'āt al 'oshshāq*.

Bokhāri. *as-Sahih*. Cairo, 1378/1958-59.

Dāremi. *as-Sonan*. N.p., n.d.

Ebn al-Monawwar, Mohammad. *Asrār at-tauhid fi maqāmāt ash-Shaikh Abi Sa'id*. Ed. Dh. Safā. Fifth repr., Tehran,1361/1982.

Ebn 'Arabi. *al-Fotuhāt al-makkiya*. Beirut, n.d.

Ebn Māja. *as-Sonan*. Cairo, 1372/1952-53.

Foruzānfar, Badi'oz-Zamān. *Ahadith-e Mathnawi*. Tehran, 1347/1968.

Ghazāli, Abu Hāmed Mohammad. *Ehyā' 'olum ad-din*. Cairo, 1326/1908.

Ghazāli, Ahmad.*Sawāneh*. Ed. A. Mojāhed in *Majmu-'a-ye āthār-e fārsi-ye Ahmad Ghazāli*. Tehran, 1358/1979.

Hāfez, Shamso'd-Din Mohammad. *Diwān*. Ed. A. Anjawi Shirāzi, Tehran, 1361/1982.

Hojwiri, 'Ali ebn 'Othmān. *Kashf al-mahjub*. Ed. V.A. Zhukovsky. Leningrad, 1926.

Jāmi, 'Abdo'r-Rahmān. *Haft aurang*. Ed. M. Modarres Gilāni. Tehran, 1337/1958.

_____. *Nafahāt al-ons*. Ed. M. Tauhidipur. Tehran, 1336/1957.

Jonaid. *Fe'l-farq bain al-ekhlās wa 's-sedq*. Ed. A. H. Abdel-Kader in *The Life, Personality, and Writings of al-Junayd*. London, 1962.

Jorjāni, Mir Sayyed Sharif 'Ali ebn Mohammad.*at-Ta'rifāt*. Ed. G. Flügel. Leipzig, 1845.

Kalābādhi, Abu Bakr Mohammad. *at- Ta'arrofof le-madhhab ahl at-tasawwof*. Ed. 'A. Mahmud and T.'A. Sorur. Cairo, 1960.

Kāshāni, 'Ezzo'd-Din Mahmud. *Kashf al-wojuh al-*

ghorr le- ma āni nazm ad-dorr: Sharh tā 'iya Ebn Fāredh al-kobrā. Tehran, 1319/1901 (the edition is wrongly ascribed to 'Abdo'r-Razzāq Kāshāni).

_____. *Mesbāh al-hedāya*. Ed. J. Homā'i. Tehran, 1323/1944.

Kholāsa-ye Sharh-e Ta'arrof. Anonymous abridgement of Mohammad ebn 'Abdo'llāh Mostamli Bokhā rā'i's*Sharh at-ta'arrof* [see Kalābādhi]. Ed. A. 'A. Rajā'i. Tehran, 1349/1970.

Lāhiji, Mohammad. *Sharh-e Golshan-e rāz*. Ed. K. Sami'i. Tehran, 1337/1958.

Moslem. *as-Sahih*. Cairo, 1334/1916.

Nāser Khosrau. *S a 'ādat-nāma*. Appended to his *Diwān* edited by S.H. Taqizāda et al. Tehran, 1329/1950.

Qoshairi, Abo'l-Qāsem. *ar-Resālat al-Qoshairiya*. Ed. 'A. Mahmud and M. ebn ash-Sharif. Cairo, 1972-74; also, no editor, Cairo, 1940.

Rumi, Jalālo'd-Din. *Mathnawi*. Ed. R.A. Nicholson. 8 vols. London, 1925-40.

_____. *Kolliyāt-e Shams*. Ed. B. Foruzānfar. 10 vols. Tehran, 1336-47/1957-68.

Ruzbehān Baqli. *Mashrab al-arwāh*. Ed. N.M. Hoca. Istanbul, 1974.

Sa'di, Mosleho'd- Din ebn 'Abdo'llāh. *Bustān* . Ed. Gh. Yusofi. Tehran, 1363/1984.

Sarrāj, Abu Nasr. *al-Loma 'fe't-tasawwof*. Ed. R.A. Nicholson. London, 1914.

Shāh Ne'mato'llāh. *Resā 'el* . Ed. J. Nurbakhsh. 4 vols. Tehran, 1357/1978.

Solàmi, Abu 'Abdo'r-Rahmān. *Tabaqāt as-sufiya.* Ed.
J. Petersons. Leiden, 1960.

Soyuti. *al-Jāme 'as-saghir* (Munāwi, *Faidh al-qadir:
Sharh jāme 'as-saghir*, Beirut, 1972).

Tabrizi, Sharafo'd-Din Hosain. *Rashf al-alhāz fi kashf
al-alfāz.* Ed. N. Māyel Herawi. Tehran,
1362/1983.

Tahānawi, Mohammad. *Kashshāf estelāhāt al-fonun.* 2
vols. Calcutta, 1862.

Termedhi. *as-Sonan.* Cairo, 1357/1938.

159

Doqqi, Abu Bakr. 113,143.

Ebn 'Abbās.29.

Ebn 'Atā' Abo'l-'Abbas. (d. 922) 71, 87, 111, 148, 149.

Ebn Faurak, Abu Bakr Mohammad.129.

Ebn Jalā'. 75.

Ebn Masruq. 59.

Ebrāhim Adham. (d. 776 or 783) 22, 40, 61, 114.

Ebrāhim Khawwās see: Khawwās.

'effat, continence. 145.

Egypt. 84, 85.

ehsān, beneficence. 153, 154.

ekhlās, sincerity. 105, 106, 109.

'elm, doctrine.16, 116.

ensāf, just treatment. 90.

eqāmat, establishing. 127, 129, 134.

erādat, will. 116, 119, 126.

eshfāq, sympathy. 101.

eslām, submission. 121, 153.

estejābat, response. 19.

esteqāmat, constancy. 125, 129, 132.

'eyān, eye-witnessing. 44.

Fadhl Balkhi, Mohammad ebn. 51, 60, 128, 132.

fanā', annihilation. 16, 31, 44.

farā'edh, obligatory actions. 9, 145.

farq, dispersion. 115.

fesq, ungodliness. 11.

Fodhail ebn 'Eyādh. (d. 653) 86, 91, 109.

fojur, lewdness. 11.

ghaflat, heedlessness. 4, 8, 15, 17, 22, 24, 131.

ghair, 'other'. 16.

gnosis.15, 42, 44, 90, 115, 121, 131, 150, 153, 154.

gnostic.15, 17, 20, 29, 45, 51, 52, 58, 61, 76, 86, 90, 93, 98, 111, 115, 127, 132, 134, 149, 150, 153.

Habib 'Ajami. (8th century) 36.

Haddād, Abu Hafs. (10th century) 23, 25, 143.

hadith, prophetic tradition. 7, 10, 11, 12, 13, 18, 21, 26, 37, 38, 39, 40, 45, 62, 69, 71, 76, 91,

162

Kermānshāhi, Mozaffar. 89.

Khafif, Abu 'Abdo'llāh ebn. (d. 982) 56, 75.

khāles, pure. 109, 115.

khalwat, retreat. 23.

Kharaqāni, Abo'l-Hasan. (d. 1034) 113.

Kharrāz, Abu Sa'id. (d. 890) 38, 111.

khatā', what is wrong. 12.

khauf, fear. 42.

Khawwās, Ebrāhim. (d. 904) 42, 43.

Khedhr. 152.

kofr, unbelief. 5, 50.

Koran. 3, 5, 7, 8, 10, 12, 13, 14, 19, 20, 21, 23, 26, 28, 44, 45, 46, 50, 51, 52, 63, 64, 73, 76, 92, 93, 94, 100, 101, 107, 109, 115, 116, 118, 120, 121, 125, 126, 127, 128, 131, 132, 133, 142, 150, 151, 152, 153, 154.

Lordship, see: *robubiyat*.

ma'āsi 1, 4, 5, 6, 7, 8, 9, 11, 12, 13, 18, 21.

Maghrebi, Abu 'Othmān. 108.

Makhul. 112.

malakut, spiritual realm. 76, 100.

Mamshād Dinawari. 144.

maqām, station. 12, 49.

Mar'ashi, Hodhaifa. 111.

Mecca. 141.

Midian. 85.

mobāh, indifferent. 107.

Mobārak 'Abdo'llāh ebn. 55, 145, 146, 147.

Mohammad, see: Prophet.

mohaqqequn, realizers. 16, 20.

moharramāt unlawful things. 35, 38, 61,62, 64, 152.

mohāsabat, self-examination. 8.

Mohāsebi, Hāreth.(d. 857) 38, 110.

mojāhadat, struggle. 2, 9, 43, 129.

mokhlas, 'made sincere'. 108, 113.

mokhles, 'sincere one'. 106, 107, 113.

moktasab, earned. 25.

molk, corporeal realm. 76,

moqarrabān, those brought near to Him. 14.

163

Rumi, Maulana Jalao'd-Din. (d. 1273) 125, 139, 140.

Ruzbehān Baqli Shirazi. (d. 1209) 37, 43, 62, 89, 100, 115, 131, 149.

Ṣādeq, Imam Ja'far aṣ-. (d. 765) 23.

Sa'di, Mosleḥo'd-Din. (d. 1292) 81.

Ṣaḥiḥ of Moslem. 126.

Sahl ebn 'Abdo'llāh. (d. 896) 2, 16, 23, 39, 41, 42, 52, 73, 88, 98, 112, 113, 114.

San'ā'. 83.

Sanjān, Moḥammad ebn. 72.

Saqaṭi, Sari. (d. 855 or 857) 53, 60, 141, 142, 145.

Sarrāj, Abu Naṣr. (d. 988) 143.

sawāb, what is right. 12.

Sayyāri, Abo'l-'Abbās. 22.

ṣeddiqān, the righteous. 108.

ṣedq, truthfulness. 105.

serr, inmost consciousness. 3, 4, 5, 12, 43, 76, 99, 100, 101, 127, 144.

servanthood, see: 'obudiyat.

Shāh Kermāni. (d. after 880) 71.

Shāh Ne'mato'llāh Wali. (d. 1430) 62, 132, 150, 151.

shahādat, professing the faith. 126.

Shaibān, Ebrāhim ebn. 41.

Shaqiq Balkhi, see Balkhi.

shari'at. 1, 9, 22, 20, 107, 125, 131, 134, 144, 145, 149, 150, 151, 152.

Shebli. (d. 945) 11, 37, 39, 40, 56, 82, 128, 129.

sherk, associating anything with God. 2, 69, 76, 109, 114.

shobohāt, doubtful things. 35, 37, 38, 40, 41, 42.

Shuniziya Mosque. 142.

sincerity. 17, 19, 21, 76.

Sofyān Thauri. 42, 58.

sonnat, the Prophet's Custom. 110, 121, 133, 145.

stability. 90.

state. 73, 77, 86, 92, 107, 108, 116, 117, 118, 119, 126, 134, 139,

143, 151, see also: *ḥāl*.

station. 13, 14, 28, 61, 74, 86, 90, 91, 92, 100, 127, 139, 144, 149, see also: *maqām*.

subsistence. 89, see also: *baqā.'*

ṭā'at, obedience. 4, 5, 12, 14, 17, 18, 20, 25, 28, 29.

Tamimi, 'Abdo'llāh ebn 'Ali ebn Moḥammad at-. 24.

tamkin, stability.17, 44.

taqwā, wariness. 69, 73.

taqwim, setting up. 127, 134.

tauḥid, Divine Unity. 76, 119.

tawādho', humility. 81.

tawakkol, trust, 41.

ṭā'wil, interpretation. 42.

Termedhi, Moḥammad ebn 'Ali. (d. 932) 99.

unbelief, see: *kofr*.

Wābesa. 39.

wājedun, finders. 17.

waqt, present moment. 28, 45, 101, 144.

wara', abstinence. 35.

Wāseti, Abu Bakr. (d. after

932) 24, 30, 57, 74, 130.

witnessing. 8, 44, 73, 76, 88, 91, 94, 99, 109, 115, 119, 121, 129, 134, 145, 153.

Yahyā ebn Mo'ādh. (d. 871-2) 30, 41, 42, 51, 54, 58, 59, 60, 87, 88, 126.

Yusof ebn Asbāṭ. (d. between 807 and 814) 36, 82.

Yusof ebn Ḥosain Rāzi. (d. 916) 58, 89, 112.

zakāt, religious tax. 151.

zinat, fancy clothing. 54.

zohd, renunciation. 54.

zohhād, renouncers. 15.